HUMANITY'S SPIRITUAL PLAGUE

Beloved Reader,

Throughout our life's journey we search for and open doors looking for responses to fulfill us. In this beautiful book I have gathered many answers that can help you live a better life knowing that hope and the love of God are always near you.

I give to you this book as an alternative choice. It will help you answer your questions and find your freedom.

HUMANITY'S SPIRITUAL PLAGUE

A SIMPLE PRACTICAL WORKBOOK ON RELEASING ADDICTIVE EARTHBOUND SPIRITS

VICTOR BARRON

The material in this book is not intended to replace orthodox medical treatment. If ailments or symptoms persist, consult a physician immediately (preferably one with a holistic medical background). The reader should use discretion and take sole responsibility when using any of the applications of the material presented.

Published By: Eagle Publishing Company

Printed in the United States of America

Library of Congress Control Number: 2002096238

Barron, Victor
Humanity's spiritual plague: a simple, practical workbook on releasing addictive earthbound spirits / Victor Barron. -- 1st ed.
p. cm.
Includes bibliographical references and index.
ISBN 0-9721598-2-7

1. Spiritual healing and spiritualism. I. Title

BF1275.F3B37 2002 133.9
QBI33-643

Cover Designs: Victor Barron

Illustrations: Victor Barron

Photography: Blanca Barron and Tony Dueñas

CONTENTS

Chapter 5

Chapter 6

Appendix

MY PERSONAL VIEW OF GOD

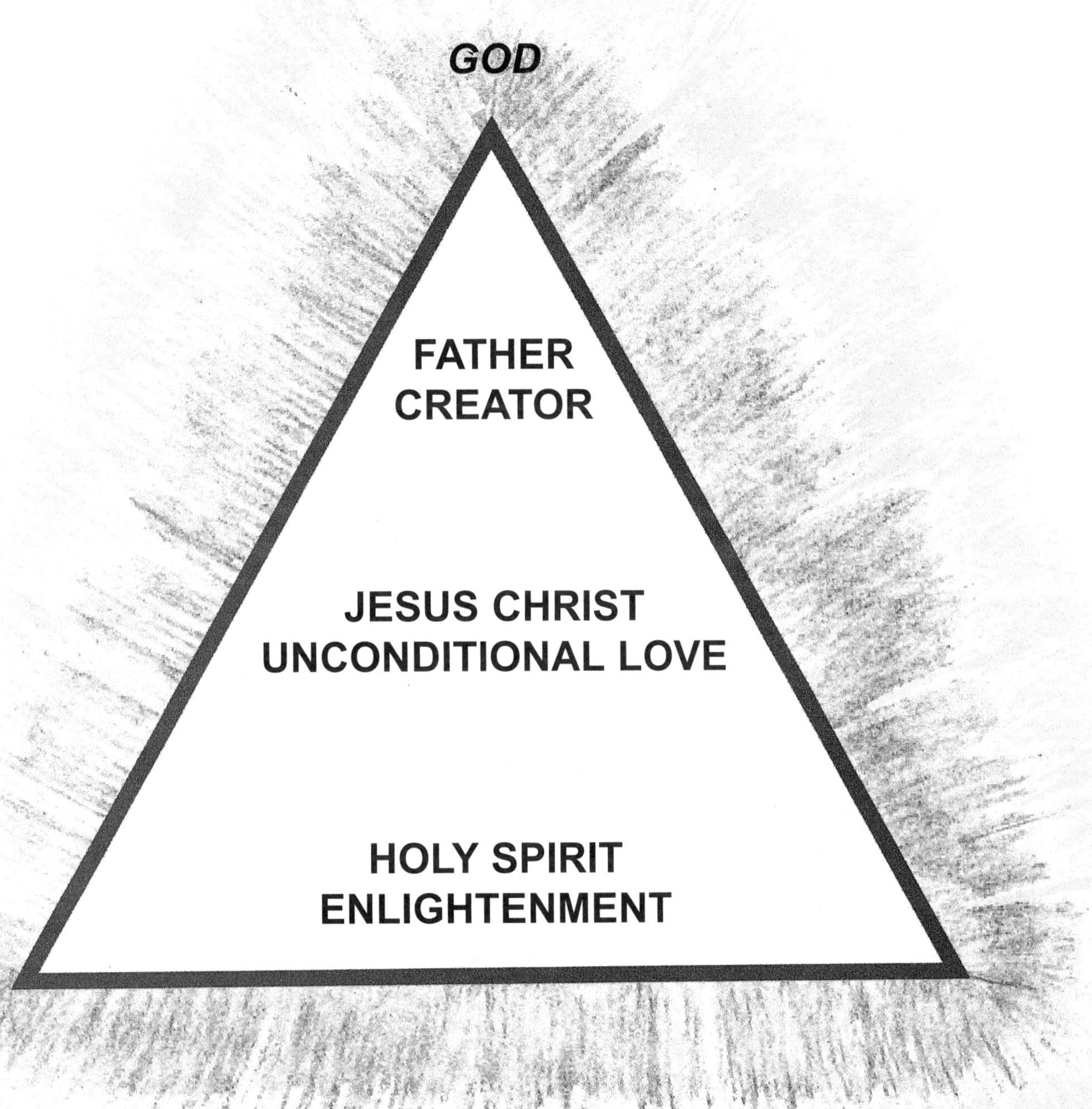

GOD IS KNOWN BY MANY NAMES

DEDICATION

I wish to dedicate this book to God my Father, my Spirit Guides, Angelic Beings and all Spiritual Teachers of high frequency in God's consciousness who have assisted, guided and protected me in all my healings and teachings.

To Lisa
Many Blessings
Victor
8-18-16

Victor Barron
Shaman
Whirling Wind

ACKNOWLEDGMENT

My dearest Blanca, I thank God for allowing us to come together as one. You give me such peace of heart and mind. Your common sense approach, quick intellect, and spiritual growth fill me with pride. I am blessed that you are my true love. The more I look at your beauty, the more I honor and respect you. You have brought such joy to me. Thank you Blanca, for your patience, love, understanding, and infinite support.

ACKNOWLEDGMENTS

I lovingly thank my parents for the understanding they gave me about life. I will always be grateful to my mother, who taught me courage and to my father, who taught me good moral values. I thank God for allowing them to continue being a part of my life.

I would also like to acknowledge my friend, Perri Curtis, who organized and typed my original notes. She assisted me by compiling, organizing, and ultimately typing my first draft.

It was an honor for me to have had the assistance of Jan McCarthy, Lucila Grijalva, Olivia Limón, and Magda Rivas, who gave unselfishly from their hearts and souls to bring this book into print. The book took precious hours away from family and friends. I do not have the words to express my profound gratitude for their total commitment and willingness to adjust their schedules.

Jerry Aguilar was instrumental in providing guidance from a layman's perspective. His knowledge and expertise in the area of editing, organizing, and formatting this book have been invaluable. Tony Dueñas' passion and commitment to photography was greatly appreciated. Blanca Barron's multiple talents, including photography, were invaluable. I would like to give special thanks to all the volunteers who participated in the photo sessions.

I would like to recognize and thank two special people for their expertise: Marisela Carlos for her spiritual-intuitive insights in regards to my book and Ernesto Grijalva for his professional grammar advice and translation skills.

To My Readers:

The ideas for this book originally came to me in first person form. I am a simple person and have always worked from my heart. As I went through the steps of bringing this material into book format, I found it overwhelming because it was such a mental process.

I wanted to simplify my work so I chose to use the masculine pronoun. Then my creativity began to flow. Please feel free to substitute the feminine pronoun "she," if this feels better.

Whenever a reference is made to *blessing* note that the healer or anyone else can ask for God's blessing through formal prayer or by expressing his own words. You can also bless (i.e. olive oil, incense, water, triangles, cross, clients, etc.).

INTRODUCTION

I wish to share with you something of my background, of who I am, my commitment to God and my spiritual work. My purpose in writing this book is to reach out and help humanity with an alternative spiritual method of healing. I would also like to bring an awareness of the spiritual world and its addictive entities that plague the human race.

For over twenty-six years I have dedicated myself to healing the sick on their spiritual, mental, emotional, and physical levels. I have also removed addictive earthbound spirits from people, their homes, work areas and wherever people are being harassed. I have inserted their spirits back into their physical bodies, as well as broken witchcraft, voodoo and spells.

As a teacher and healer I have traveled and worked in the United States, Latin America, Singapore, and Australia. I have connected people with their Guardian Angels. I have also taught energy healing, traditional spiritual Shaman healings, removal of earthbound spirits, meditations, spiritual unfoldings, retreats, and soul attunements.

All of these things have been accomplished with the grace of God, who has blessed me with Guardian Angels, spirit guides of high frequency, and the gifts of spiritual healing and ghost busting. As God's instrument, I allow my physical body to be utilized by my spirit guides who work through me to do the healings. All that I teach and do has been given to me by God to help all who are ready and willing to help themselves.

In my work as a healer, it has come to my awareness that approximately 80% of my clients have problems associated with addictive earthbound spirit attachments.

This means that a large portion of our population is not functioning to their fullest capacity as God intended. I feel compelled to teach and write about this subject because ***there is a desperate need for this knowledge****. I would also like to offer humanity a way to learn how to effectively deal with addictive earthbound spirits.*

There are many people who claim that they have the ability to do this type of work, but in actuality they do not have the spiritual strength. ***Please do not misunderstand.*** *This is not to say that there aren't others in the world with the same ability or who are even better than I. Throughout my travels I have yet to meet someone with the same gifts and the desire to share them.*

I asked for God's guidance in helping me train other healers in places where I was unable to visit. I was then given instructions and techniques to give to those wishing to be of service to God the Father. I have been teaching these techniques for the past seven years. Now this information is being passed on to you in this book.

Personal Backgound

I was born in California of Mexican parents and received a strict Catholic upbringing. I can remember in my early childhood my paternal grandmother, who lived with us. She would sit and speak to me about God and my Guardian Angel. Grandmother had plenty of time to teach me. She taught me how to bless myself. I remember how hard it was for me to make the sign of the cross. I would practice making the sign of the cross over and over.

My parents and grandmother instilled within me a strong sense of values. From

an early age I began to experience an inner knowing of my spiritual path. All I ever wanted was to be in God's presence. I loved going to our parish church which was two blocks away. I often attended Mass up to three times on a Sunday. I would sit up front and if I had a choice I would stay there all day. The presence of God for me was always intense and loving. My calling to serve God was so strong during adolescence that I even considered joining the priesthood, but God had other plans for me.

I have always felt very close to God. I attended morning and after school Mass, and of course, Sunday Mass. On special occasions when missionaries visited our parish, I would attend an evening Mass. I recall that during one of these evening Masses, I felt an overwhelming pull and calling to receive the Holy Sacrament of Communion. I was not aware of what Holy Communion was. I must have been five or six years of age when my hunger to receive God was irresistible.

I remember walking towards the altar. All the adults were staring at me with bewilderment. Their stares made me feel very nervous and uneasy, but I continued. When I arrived at the altar the missionary priest stopped and looked at me as if to say, "What are you doing?" I looked into his eyes and he looked into mine. He bent towards me and whispered for me to open my mouth and receive the Body of Christ. The moment I heard this, I felt relaxed and a big smile came over my face. I had received the Holy Eucharist for the first time.

My heart felt so warm and my body was light as I ran home. I felt I was flying. I could not wait to get home to tell my mother what I had experienced. The next thing I remember, after my natural high with God, was my mother's concern about how I could have done something so "wrong." She rushed me back to see the parish priest. He advised me not to do this again until I was ready to receive the Sacrament of First Holy Communion.

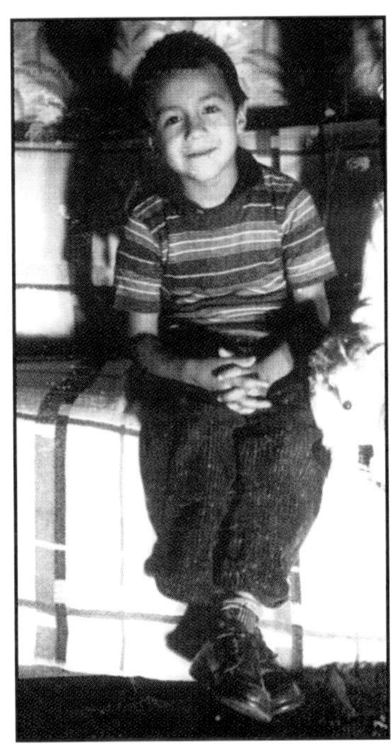

My first five years of school were spent in a parochial school. I ultimately completed my education in the public school system. I was a very active child who couldn't sit still for any length of time. At home my parents only spoke Spanish while at school all my lessons were taught in English. These two factors made learning difficult for me. The one thing that I found rewarding in parochial school was learning the Lord's prayer and the Hail Mary, which were said several times daily.

Every night before bedtime I would pray for at least one hour. I would first talk to God then I would repeat the Lord's prayer and Hail Marys. I loved praying, it felt so good. Praying came easily for me and it gave me tremendous peace. The words and feelings would just flow out spontaneously from deep inside of me. I felt great after praying. Sometimes I would repeat the prayers hundreds of times or until I fell asleep. I prayed for everyone, especially for all the souls in purgatory.

I would like to digress for a moment and explain the importance of prayer. For many years I felt happy and content not praying as fervently. All the prayers I had uttered during childhood were accumulated blessings that saw me through many trials and tribulations. In 1989, I began to feel as though my cup of blessings was starting to dwindle. By 1994, I felt that my cup was nearly depleted so I once again began to pray more fervently. I felt that by praying I was able to maintain a constant connection with God, who is my strength, and who had always provided me with direction.

It is very important that children are encouraged to pray to God from an early age so that they develop a relationship with God, who will help them through the rest of their lives. Praying is a way of stockpiling blessings for the future. When young children in their innocence pray, God blesses them.

Besides praying a lot, my childhood was fairly normal. Between the ages of six and eight I spent a lot of time playing by myself in my backyard. I would spend hours playing with my wooden blocks in a tunnel-like structure I had made out of boxes. Sometimes while playing in the tunnel I would fall asleep for hours. It was during this sleep time that I became aware of voices communicating with me. Each voice was different. I identified each voice by a certain feeling and tone. I was unable to see them but I listened, talked and played with them. I listened to them more than anyone or anything else and was taught lessons about life, forgiveness, and love. I was also given instructions on how to be a good person and how to love God. Many other times I can recall laughing and playing with someone. The voice was very clear and would say, "Come on let's play." It did not bother me that I could not see anyone because it felt so natural. I now realize I was learning "to trust without the gift of sight." For the next few years my backyard brought a lot of peace to me as I played.

At the age of ten I discovered my Guardian Angel. I saw a glimpse of his wings for the first time. They were so beautiful that I wanted to fly with him. Shortly after this experience, I had my first out-of-body flight. I knew that I was going to fly, so I climbed to the roof of our house. I was disappointed because many cables and electrical lines crossed over the rooftop, and for a ten-year-old that looked very dangerous.

In bed that night, I prayed extra hard and waited for my family to fall asleep. While waiting I closed my eyes and dozed off. I woke up with the movement of my arms. They were flapping up and down at my sides, which helped me float out of my body. I continued flapping my arms up and down and realized I had gone through the ceiling and was on top of the roof. I found myself desperately trying to avoid all the electrical lines and cables. I was concerned because I had seen pigeons fly into the wires causing them to break a wing and sometimes die.

Once clear of the wires, I noticed that the faster my arms moved, the faster and higher I was able to fly. It was a new experience for me. Looking down, I quickly estimated that I was 300 to 500 feet above the ground, and I was afraid to go any higher. I floated around but always kept an eye on my home. When I came back down I was shocked to see my physical body still in bed. I had assumed my body was with me. It was then that I realized I was out of my physical body.

The next morning I rushed to school wanting the day to end quickly. I could not wait for evening to come so I could again experience my flight. When I arrived home from school, I looked around for some string to tie the wires closer together. I didn't want them interfering with my flight. I climbed to the roof with a ladder I had built and using laces from my tennis shoes managed to tie clusters of cables and wires. This gave me space to maneuver myself out safely without fear of being entangled.

One evening, my father spanked me for being mischievous and sent me to bed. As I was crying, I talked to God. Then, I prayed the rosary and fell asleep. Again I left my body. I was able to maneuver around the cables and lines fairly well, but this time I over did it. My arms felt very tired and heavy. When I stopped moving my arms, I panicked. At that moment an eagle flew up beside me, looked straight into my eyes and said, "Follow me. Do as I do." I spread my arms and soared with the eagle, flying effortlessly. It felt so different and beautiful. From that moment on I was able to fly without flapping my arms.

On another occasion I went to sleep for 10-20 minutes. I left my body and went straight up into the sky and suddenly found myself inside a plane. There I saw a sick girl who was about thirteen or fourteen years old. She had leg braces and appeared to have polio. I felt so sad for her and wanted to help. I gave her some healing and then quickly returned to my body. When I woke up I told my mother what had just happened. My mother was so excited she called my aunt to share my experience.

During my school-age years my heart was never in school. Therefore, my academic work was poor. My mother and father were not very happy. The pressure weighed heavily upon my shoulders. Even though I would try, I could never catch up with my studies.

My connection with the spiritual world was far more important to me. My Guardian Angel and another voice taught me to listen and to observe a lot of different things. They taught me to trust and to forgive. Actually, they were grooming me for my later years as a teacher. The disciplines I learned were lessons not taught at school or home. I knew that I could ask my Guardian Angel and the voices for assistance, but ***I never abused this privilege****.*

Only once did I ask my Guardian Angel and the voices for assistance. I wanted to join the Reserve Officers Training Corps but my medical exam showed that I had a hernia. The doctor, therefore, failed my application. I wanted to join so badly that I asked my guidance to please help me. My guidance told me to go back to the school doctor, which I did. This time the doctor found nothing wrong with me. He opened a new file and approved my application to join the R.O.T.C.

Between thirteen and sixteen years of age, I continued to pray, attend church, and occasionally I did a healing on someone. One time I went with a friend to visit his family in Montebello. There I met and talked with a gentleman. As I shook his hand I knew and felt he had a lot of pain in his body, especially his legs. He explained that the pain was so severe at times that he had to crawl from one room to another. While just standing there talking to him the healing process began. The man asked, "What are you doing to me? I feel your hands on my body and legs." He was in awe because I was standing about five feet from him as the pain was leaving him. When we finished talking I asked him if I could wash my hands. He led me into an area where I could wash. My guidance prompted me to ask him, "Isn't this what you've been asking for?" He replied, "I've been praying to God to help me with my pain, and you show up." I then asked him, "Don't you have God in your room?" He replied, "follow me," and he led me into a room where there was a shrine dedicated to God.

My turning point came at age seventeen, after high school graduation, when I enlisted in the United States Marine Corp. During this time I recall asking for help from God and spirits of light. There were numerous instances where they protected and guided me. Once released from active duty I felt a great compassion towards humanity. I wanted to use my gift of healing that God had entrusted to me. At the same time, I began experiencing the channeling of my spirit guides through my physical body. These spirit guides of high frequency were given to me by God. I began to realize that I was able to do many things. However, healing of the spiritual body became my favorite.

For the past twenty-six years I have been given the opportunity to work closely with my spirit guides, thus giving clients the opportunity to choose a higher and better quality of life. Every healing I do gives me more knowledge on all levels.

No one on this planet knows it all. We are always learning. We are all teachers. I am a simple man. I do not profess to have command of the English language nor am I a "motivational speaker." I will give it to you straight and simple. ***THERE IS NO MORE TIME TO WASTE.***

It has been a dream of mine for many years to write a simple workbook. This workbook is intended to bring an awareness to what I call "Humanity's Spiritual Plague" — LEECHES. They are addictive earthbound spirits who can create havoc in people's lives. Approximately 80% of the population has some sort of spirit attachment.

This book will show those wanting to help humanity a far safer way to assist people. You do not have to be a clairvoyant or medium to do leech removal. However, you must have the gifts of unconditional love, compassion, and humility, as well as faith in God. A faith, which in turn, gives you the spiritual strength to help humanity.

SEE WITH THE EYES OF YOUR HEART,
NOT YOUR MIND

CHAPTER ONE

THE SPIRITUAL PLAGUE

At this time in history the human population is being attacked by what I call the "Spiritual Plague." As previously mentioned, approximately 80% of our world population is currently affected by addictive earthbound spirits. Addictive earthbound spirits (leeches) are trapped spirits. They are in a no-zone where lower frequency spirits exist. These spirits do not have the spiritual strength to elevate themselves to the frequency / zone / consciousness into which they are required to go. Therefore, they end up in this no-zone / earthbound state of consciousness.*

These addictive earthbound spirits are unable to reincarnate. The rate that people reincarnate is slowing down. In my opinion, this is due to the new order of consciousness now entering the planet. With this higher consciousness coming in, these low-frequency spirits are not being given the opportunity for a new body. They are unable to enter and experience the physical world in the normal fashion.

Addictive earthbound spirits are currently feeding upon the human race. This is because of the negative thought forms we produce within our consciousness. Leeches are attracted to human beings, their minds, and all places and things that generate magnetic energy fields.

All the negative energy thought patterns we create produce negative waves of energy on our mental, physical, emotional, and spiritual bodies. This leaves us open and vulnerable to the abundant number of addictive earthbound spirits who are trapped here on the planet.

---

* Addictive Earthbound Spirits, also known as Leeches, are human beings who are now in spirit form and desire to continue to experience their negative human tendencies by attaching themselves to a host body (human being).

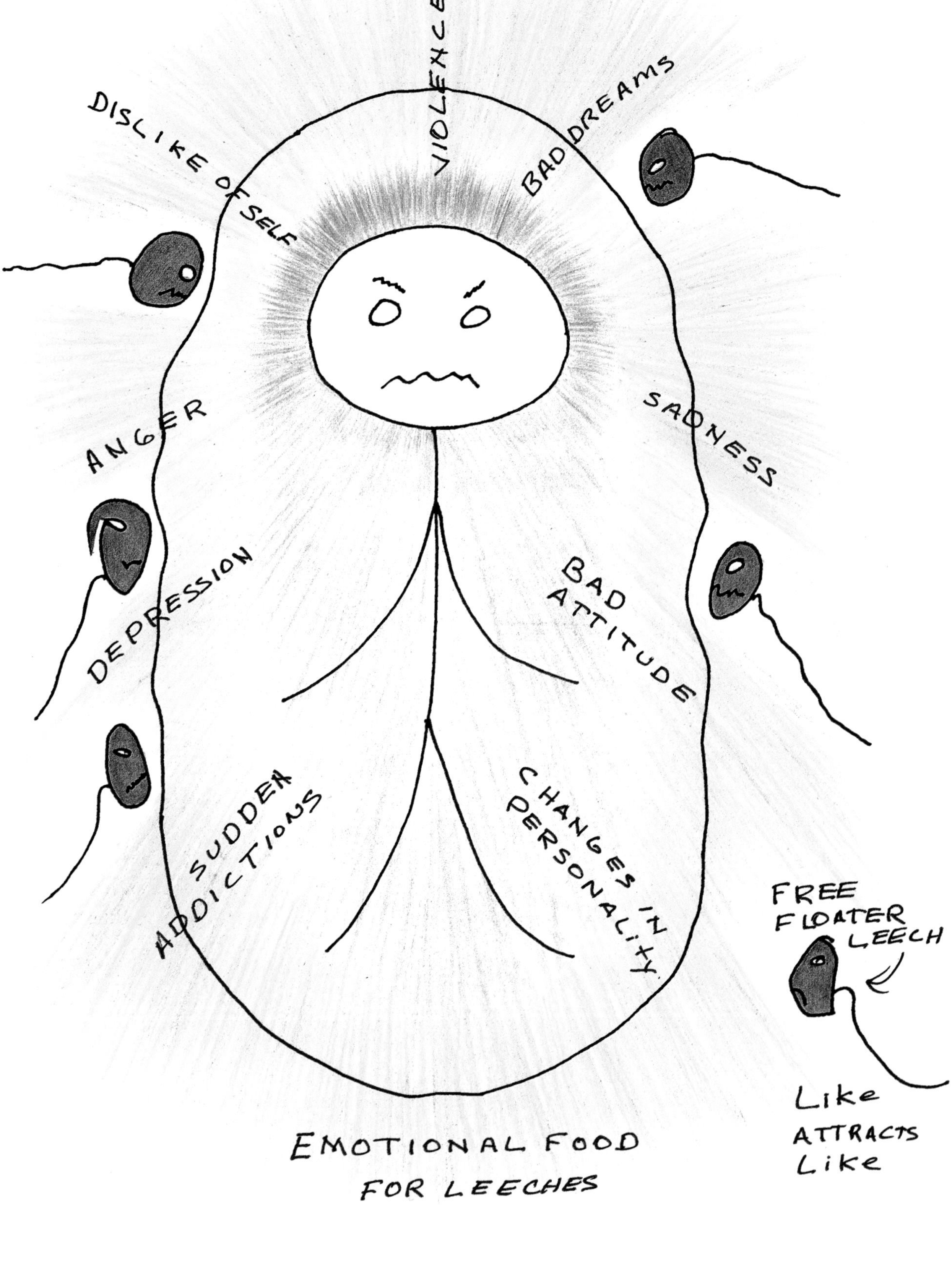

DISLIKE OF SELF
VIOLENCE
BAD DREAMS
ANGER
SADNESS
DEPRESSION
BAD ATTITUDE
SUDDEN ADDICTIONS
CHANGES IN PERSONALITY
FREE FLOATER LEECH
Like ATTRACTS Like

EMOTIONAL FOOD FOR LEECHES

Leeches are baited by our negative thoughts. We, as human beings, are constantly moving magnetic energy throughout our physical body—our mind being the biggest conductive unit of energy. Every time we get angry or display a BAD ATTITUDE we are opening a pathway that attracts negative energies to our energy field. With continued anger and a BAD ATTITUDE we end up with a leech who will ultimately attach itself to us or embed itself within one of our chakras. The mere fact that we are in human form makes us all susceptible to leeches. NO ONE IS IMMUNE to this problem — NO ONE. It can happen to anyone.

In our modern day surroundings, we are constantly bombarded with magnetic energy from microwaves, air conditioners, motor vehicles, cell phones, computers, and electrical appliances. The magnetic energy fields grow daily because technological devices are being offered at more affordable prices. Consequently, the problem of addictive earthbound spirits is magnified as the number and availability of these devices increases.*

Have you noticed how your own children and perhaps even yourselves have become addicted to the various computer games and internet activities now available to computer users?

If you are a parent I would strongly recommend that you pay close attention to your children's behavior if they play on computers. If they show signs of antisocial behavior, exhibit a bad attitude, are argumentative or have bad dreams these are signs that your child is in need of a healing.

One commonality that exists between radio and television is that they both

---

* Notes From The Cosmos p. 102

increase negative thought patterns in individuals. The negative programs, violence, derogatory and suggestive language used on television, radio, videos and films register as an intense distorted frequency. This frequency increases the rate of negative thought patterns within our subconscious minds. Continual exposure to this subtle negative programming amplifies these negative thought forms until they reach a dangerous level.

When certain stressful situations arise these "overloaded" individuals react in a negative way. In essence, we no longer take the time to process information and events through our hearts, where the real truth can be found. We simply react.

Our negative thought forms and all the technological devices that we use daily generate more and more magnetic energy fields. These magnetic fields have now opened the doors to many negative influences including addictive earthbound spirit attachment.

How Do We Protect Ourselves Against Leech Attachments?

- *Love God*
- *Love yourself*
- *Pray*
- *Grow in consciousness*
- *Keep a positive attitude*
- *Be joyful*
- *Be happy*
- *Maintain balance in all levels of your life (see illustration)*

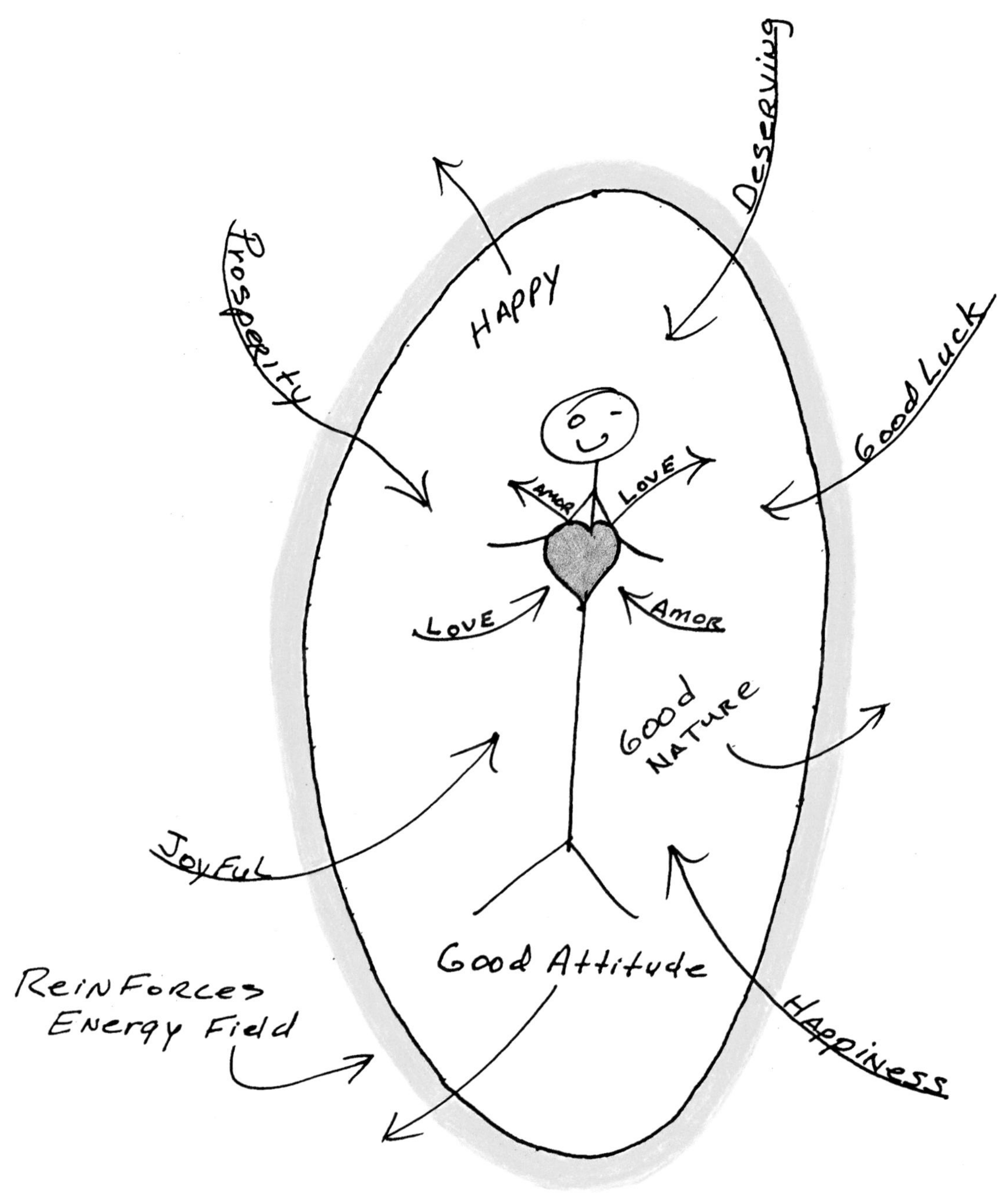

Maintain balance in all Levels of your Life

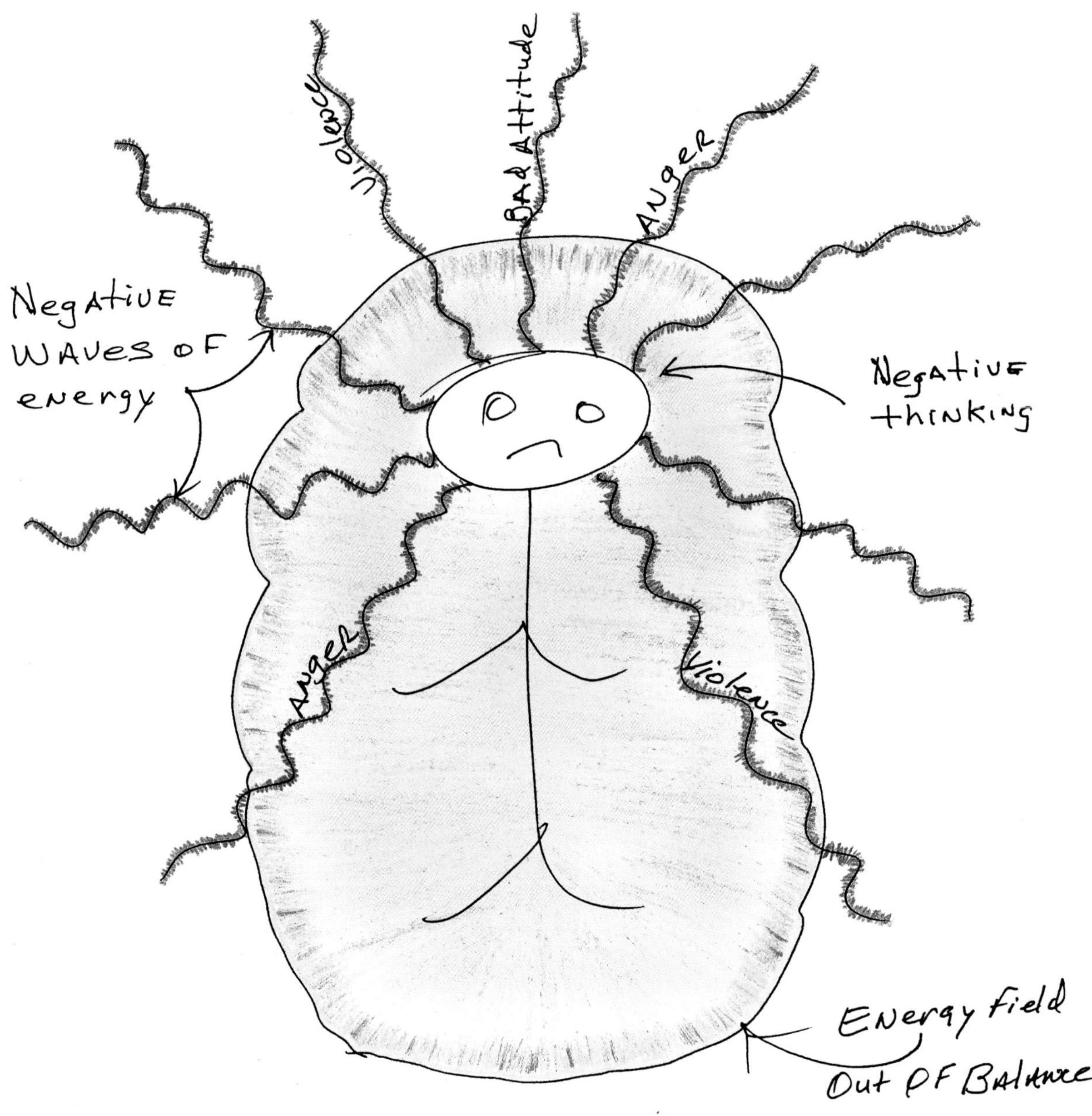

Our conscious and subconscious mind creates negative waves of energy, which produces imbalances within our energy field. This causes the aura to wobble and weaken making us vulnerable to negative leech attachments.

An individual's energy field goes into a wobble and becomes weak when they have a negative emotional outburst. It is at this time, that the person becomes vulnerable to leech attachments. Negative waves of energy are released by the individual. Once these waves of energy extend beyond the energy field they travel and any free-floater that recognizes negative frequencies, such as anger, bad attitude, etc., can then trace these waves back to the point of origin. In this case, the host body is acting as a negative human generator.

Each time an individual has a negative outburst the leeches who can recognize that particular energy begin to surround the person. The leeches attach themselves to a host body to reexperience their negative human tendencies.

Once attached, the leeches can continuously disrupt the individual's thinking. This disruption causes conflict and eventually anger. Every time the leeches feed on the negative energy, they become stronger and hold more control over the emotions of the host body.

Note: Leeches do not produce negative waves. They ARE the attitude or negativity within themselves.

NOTES

UNCONDITIONAL LOVE

Chapter 1.1

WHY I CALL THEM LEECHES

*I call earthbound spirits "leeches" for the simple fact that they remind me of a small bloodsucking worm. The more clients I treat with similar symptoms the more I realize how they cling and prey upon individuals with the same negative attitude and mental thinking. These addictive earthbound spirits are starving for negative emotions and addictions. Remember—***like attracts like***. The strongest attachment is on our spinal cord (the power cord). Most of our body's vital force travels in this area, which is why it is an ideal place for a leech to live. From this point the leech or leeches are able to move freely causing more interference on your mental, emotional, physical, and spiritual levels. When I perceive these dark human shadows, they appear to have a banana-like form or shape.*

They are human in nature with all negative addictions, attitudes, and personalities; but they are in spirit form. They live and are able to maintain themselves within the host body. They cannot leave. The ways in which they can leave are: the host dies, experiences electrical shock or receives a healing from a qualified healer. These healers must have the spiritual strength to help the leeches on their journey to another dimension or consciousness in which they belong.

No one is immune to leech attachment. Light workers, spiritual healers, clergy, body workers, energy transferrers, counselors, health practitioners, lay persons — everyone is vulnerable.

Chapter 1.2

LEECH AND SPIRIT LEVELS

Below, I have categorized leeches and spirits by levels. The description in level one (1) is that of free-floaters. Levels two (2) through four (4) describes spirits that attach themselves to the host body. Levels five (5) and six (6) are best left to those specializing in exorcism.

LEVEL 1

In this beginning level many people feel that every lost soul, given the opportunity, will run to the light. This is not so. Only those receptive leeches/spirits will run, skip, and jump into the light when a white candle is lit and they are asked to leave. Many people can give this act of unconditional love and compassion in sending leeches to the light.

LEVEL 2

Leeches of this level wish to go to the light. However, they need assistance in order to be released from the client's energy field. We must keep in mind that the longer the leech remains attached to the host body, the greater the aggravation and stress for both the client and the leech.

LEVEL 3

Leeches of this level are addictive. Sometimes they are departed relatives, spouses or significant others. These spirits cannot accept that they have passed into the spirit world and no longer possess a physical body. These leeches are not easily convinced and are not willing to go to the light.

Attachment to the host body is the beginning of many disruptions on all levels of a person's life. The healers must be prepared and have the spiritual strength to begin and finish the job of removing the leeches from the host body and guide them into the light.

If the healers fail in their first attempt, it becomes a much more challenging situation for all involved. By this time the leeches are well aware of the healer's and client's intention.

Thus, in future attempts, the leeches will work harder against the healer. The host body may find the whole situation overwhelming. As you can see, each level of leech removal becomes more difficult.

LEVEL 4

Leeches of this level have stronger addictions and very low frequencies. YOU, as a healer, will feel intimidated by them. The client may say to you that he feels compelled to physically strike you. He may express an unwillingness to be touched by you and demonstrate a bad attitude. He may also exhibit a deep piercing stare — as if to say, "Make me go from my host body (comfort zone)."

LEECHES ARE SPIRITS, BUT NOT ALL SPIRITS ARE LEECHES AND/OR ADDICTIVE

LEVEL 5

These spirits are sent to a host body by someone who has paid money to hurt them by means of witchcraft, voodoo, etc. The low frequency spirits at this level can disrupt an individual person or a whole family. These spirits do not wish to go to the light. If you try to assist a person who has this type of problem, ***be careful*** *or you will find yourself being molested by these bad spirits as well!!*

Make sure you find a genuine, qualified, spiritual healer who has the spiritual strength to remove these spirits and break any spell or witchcraft.

LEVEL 6

Spirits at this level are also known as the **dark force**. *These dark spirits must be respected for who they are. Never laugh or joke about this matter. It is at this level that you find total spirit possession.*

*Even though this situation is not common, it should be left to those specialized spiritual healers who have experience dealing with this level of consciousness.**

NEVER, NEVER, *challenge leeches or negative spirits regardless of their level. Such a challenge will provide a source of negativity, which will feed them, thus making them stronger. This strength can then be used against you. If further provoked, these spirits will call on their "BIG BROTHERS."*

It is easier to get their cooperation through unconditional love and compassion than through aggression and challenge. This loving approach works because it is non-threatening and allows spirits or leeches to leave of their own free will, rather than be forced to go. Be aware that spirits can attach themselves to material objects and places.

Please contact a genuine, spiritual healer that specializes in these levels. Ask for qualifications and references. ***Do not assume that all spiritual healers have this gift of spirit removal.***

---

* A qualified Spiritual Healer Chap. 1.8

NOTES

UNCONDITIONAL LOVE

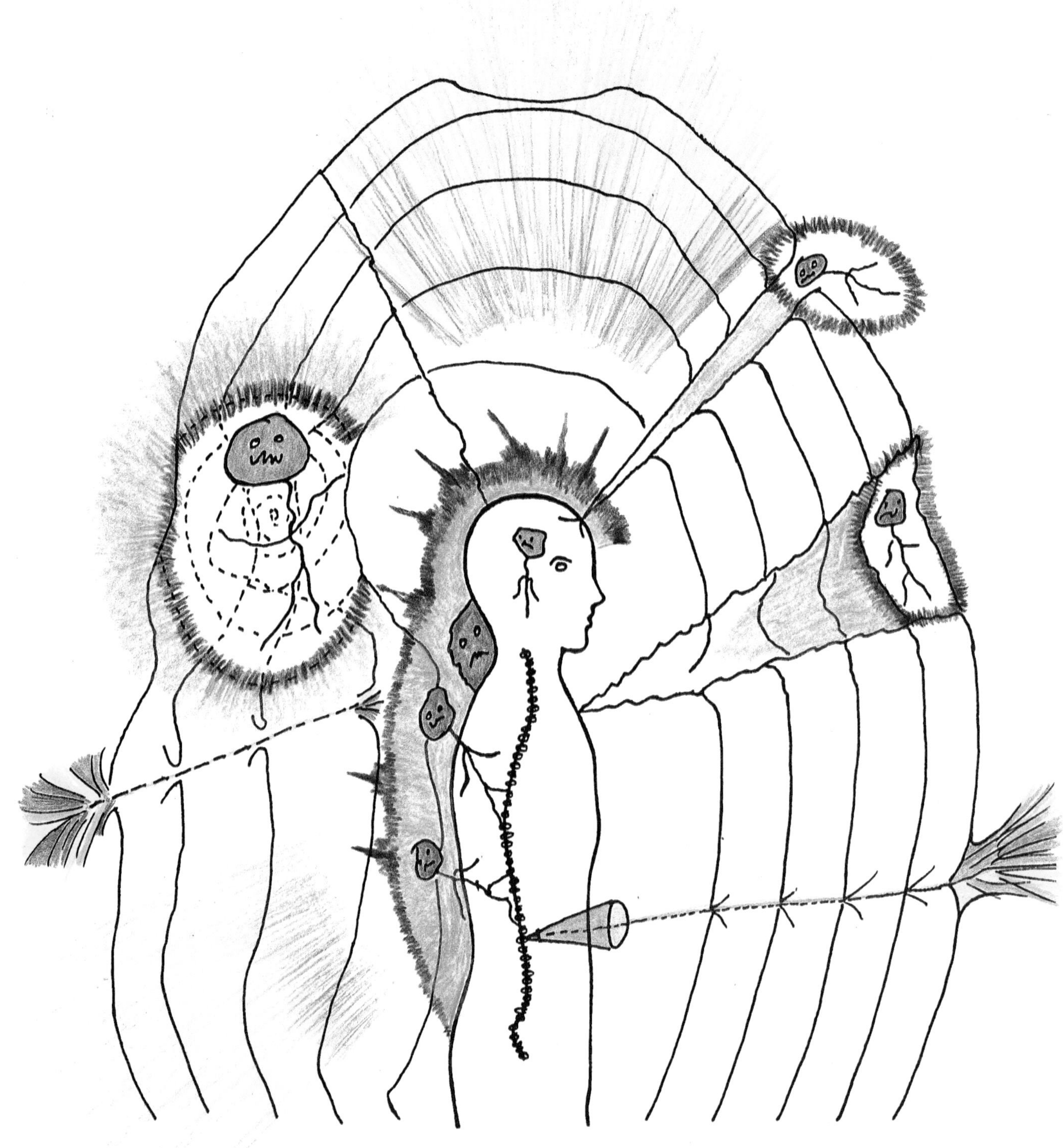

Chapter 1.3

HOW LEECHES ATTACH THEMSELVES TO PEOPLE

We, as human beings, are surrounded by an invisible luminous energy field, most commonly known as the "aura." It is our negative thought forms that first allow leeches to come into direct contact with us. As the leeches begin attaching themselves to the energy field they cause imbalances and distortions. These imbalances and distortions ultimately create tears and holes in the energy field. The doors are now open for further leech attachments.

It has been my experience that once the leeches have penetrated the energy field their ultimate goal is to reach what I call the power cord (spine). Here the leeches have their strongest attachments. They can now travel freely within the spine, chakras, and head area.

Chapter 1.4

WHY LEECHES ATTACH THEMSELVES

We, as human beings, carry within ourselves a gift that has been given to us by God! This gift is Freedom of Choice. When we choose to be negative in our thoughts and actions, we display a negative attitude, which will then open and expose us to spirit attachments.

These low frequency spirits are attracted to a host body with similar behaviors and consciousness. Most spirit attachments occur when the energy field is weak. The most common causes of spirit attachments come to individuals involved or associated with:

1. *Negative emotions*
2. *Negative mental attitude*
3. *Chemicals and drugs*
4. *Black magic, witchcraft, and spells*
5. *Physical weakness* *

These imbalances create breaks and openings in the energy field. This allows leeches to penetrate and attach themselves to different parts of the body.

---

* If you are experiencing physical weaknesses you should be careful not to involve yourself with items 1-4; otherwise you will be a prime candidate for leech attachments.

Chapter 1.5

WHAT HAPPENS WHEN YOU HAVE LEECH ATTACHMENTS

Most individuals with leech attachments will share a similar scenario. It starts with a small personality change that you may not notice. As time goes by the leeches wedge themselves into the energy field then ultimately reach the power cord (spine).

When this occurs you display huge personality and attitude changes. Generally, no one will want to be around you due to your bad attitude. You do not care to socialize with anyone, you do not speak to your friends. You'd rather be alone. This loneliness brings depression, followed by being negative, having bad dreams, and being unable to sleep well at night.

As time progresses you will experience most or all of the symptoms associated with leech attachment (see Symptom Chart on p. 45). The longer they remain with you the more disruptive your life becomes.

You grow weaker and your common sense is distorted. You are unable to differentiate between right and wrong. To individuals experiencing this state of consciousness, any choice is a good choice — even suicide. You don't have to get to this level of despair. Seek help! God will always open a door, ***if you ask****.*

WE ARE ALL PRECIOUS TO GOD!

Like Attracts Like

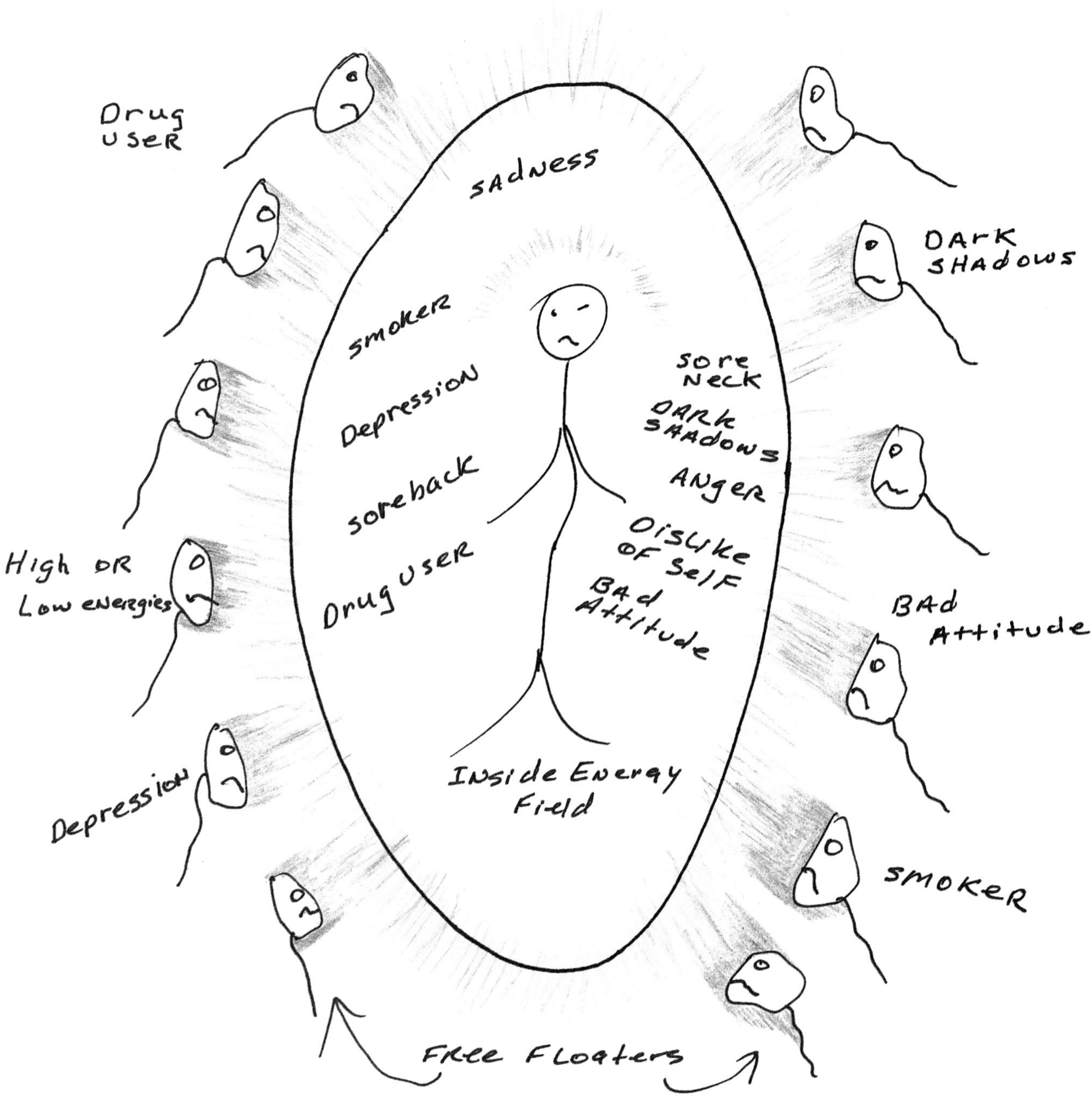

Leeches Outside Energy Field

Chapter 1.6

COMMON SYMPTOMS OF LEECH ATTACHMENT

Addictive earthbound spirits/leeches, can cause many problems in varying degrees of emotional, mental, physical, and spiritual symptoms.

Listed below are a few of the **most common symptoms** *that I frequently encounter in my workshops and healings:*

1. *Anti-social behavior*
2. *Prolonged sadness*
3. *Changes in personality*
4. *Violence*
5. *Sudden addictions*
6. *Sore back and spine*
7. *Bad dreams*
8. *Dark shadows*
9. *High or low energies*
10. *Sore neck and head*
11. *Depression*
12. *Argumentative*
13. *Ill or fatigued*
14. *Seeing grayish colors (eyes closed)*
15. *Suicidal tendencies*
16. *Piercing stare*
17. *Physical pain (sudden or on-going)*

These symptoms are the same whether the leeches are attached to the energy field, in the chakras or deep inside the spinal cord. When leeches penetrate and attach themselves inside a chakra or the spinal cord, they have a stronger hold and control over the host body. The symptoms and pain they create are far more intense and they now have the ability to move around freely within the host body. When the leeches burrow their way into the host body, the client's spirit is pushed out. This spiritual trauma is so intense that its effect is felt on the emotional, mental, physical, and spiritual levels.

Leeches that have attached themselves to the outer energy field cause the same symptoms to the host body, but the feelings are not as intense. Sometimes people are unaware of who they really are and therefore, are unable to detect that there is something drastically wrong with them.

Removing leeches from within a chakra or the spinal cord has to be done with great spiritual strength, faith, and guidance. If you do not succeed in removing them from their comfort zone, the leeches will burrow in deeper making it more difficult to remove them. As a result, more pain and discomfort is felt by the client. The leeches can even prevent the client from coming back for further treatment.

It is important to note that when you start a healing you must ensure that you are capable of treating the client. **Listen** *very carefully to your inner guidance.* **Do not proceed if you are incapable of completing the treatment.** *By all means, do not leave the client worse off than when you started. Should you encounter this problem, make sure you have a backup team to help you. Do not create bad karma for yourself by doing the wrong things to others. If you know that you cannot help your client with the proper treatment, please have integrity and do the right thing.*

Refer them to a healer who ***is*** *capable.*

God has designed a safety clause for all of us. I call this clause the "window period." In my years of working with students and healers I have noticed that when these individuals are in their window periods they will receive many clients.*

As a healer begins to develop healing skills, he will draw to himself those individuals that he is capable of helping. Based upon his capabilities, the healer should determine whether the client requires an individual or group healing. He needs to use common sense when making this decision. ***"My Father in heaven will send to you that which you are capable of giving."***

All healing situations that come are windows of opportunity. They allow for growth in faith, consciousness, love for humanity, and for building spiritual strength.

CAUTION: DENIAL OF SYMPTOMS — As a healer, be aware of clients who deny all symptoms and prepare yourself for the worst. The Leech Test is very important because there is always an exception. (See Chap. 3)

---

* Window period- stepping into a period of awakening spiritually.

Chapter 1.7

CAN LEECHES BE REMOVED?

Yes, leeches can be removed. There are many different techniques for releasing and removing leeches. With God's blessing and the teachings of my Spirit Guides I was taught how to develop many methods to provide leech removal for my clients.

I saw an overwhelming need to help humanity. I prayed to God for a safe method that everyone could use to remove leech attachments, while still maintaining good spiritual healer-hygiene. God answered my prayer. He gave me simple instructions to teach those with a ***passion*** *how to remove and release leeches.*

HEALING PROCESS FOR REMOVING UNWANTED ADDICTIVE EARTHBOUND SPIRITS (LEECHES)

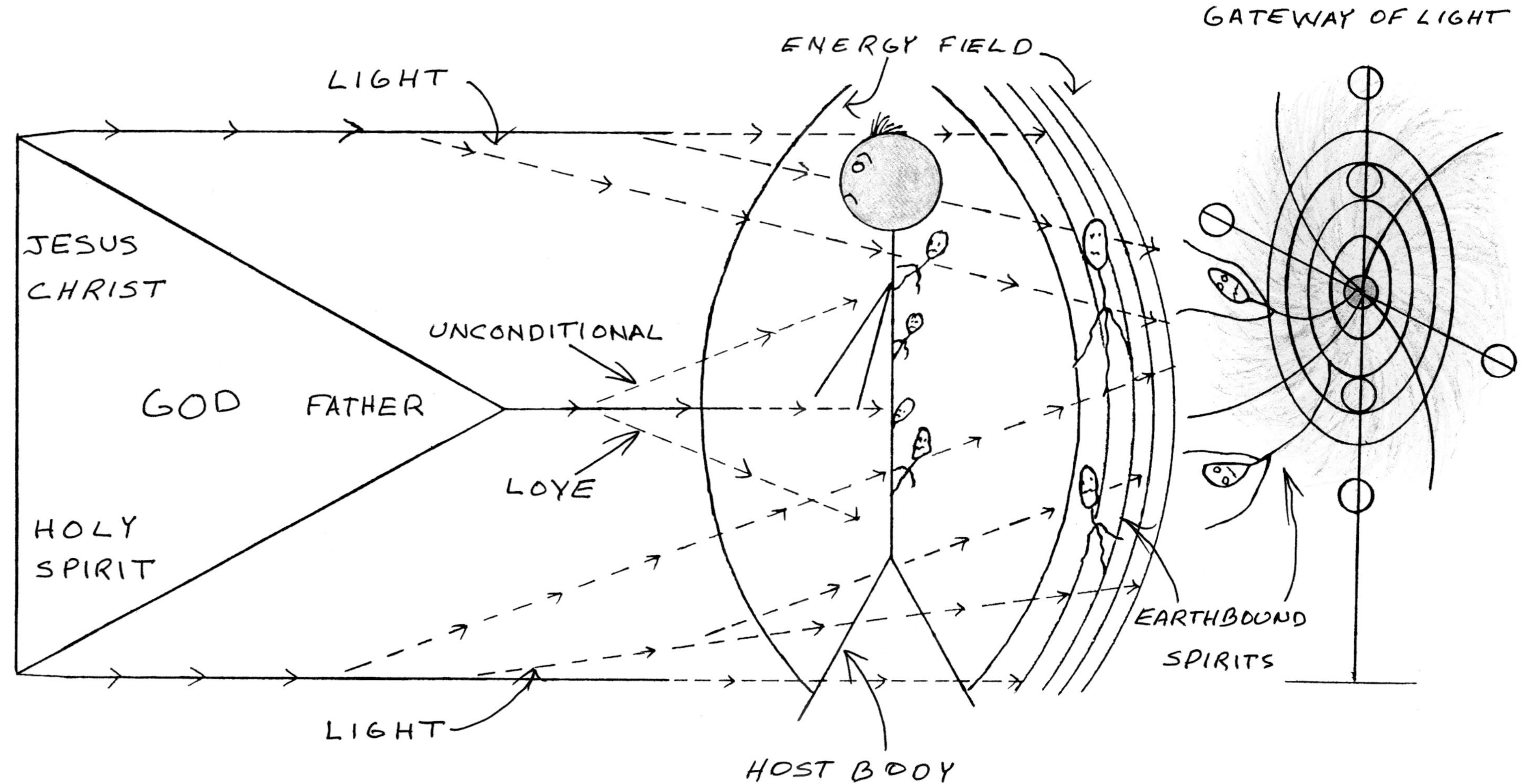

LEECHES ARE REMOVED FROM THE HOST BODY AND PULLED INTO THE VORTEX OF THE HOLY CROSS.

Chapter 1.8

CAN ANY HEALER REMOVE LEECHES?

No! Not all healers can remove leeches. Many healers have beautiful healing gifts. However, ***only*** *those healers who have the* <u>*following*</u> *will be able to remove leeches:*

- *A great love for God*
- *Love for self*
- *Unconditional love for humanity*
- *Love for the spiritual world*

They will also have:

- *A knowing*
- *A natural thirst*
- *An inner feeling or calling*

I desire that all be knowledgeable in this area of spirituality so that they will not be afraid of what they cannot see or understand. My workshops and group training sessions are designed for everyone. This information that I give to you will empower you and give you hope. Always remember that God's help is nearby. ***Simply ask.***

Chapter 1.9

WHAT HAPPENS TO LEECHES AFTER REMOVAL?

In my Leech Removal Workshop, I teach that healers are responsible for maintaining a clean healing area. A clean area means that, after removing leeches from a client, the leeches are not left in a state of limbo or allowed to become free-floaters. Remember, once a leech is set free, they can easily cause more harm by reattaching themselves to you, your client or any other vulnerable human being. This is why all leeches are given the opportunity to enter the porthole of light, which consists of seven frequencies. The porthole that I use is the Holy Cross.***

God is unconditional love, illumination, and hope. Once the Holy Cross is blessed and activated, it acts as a huge vacuum. During leech removal, leeches are pulled into the Holy Cross before being hurled into their frequency or state of consciousness. This process gives them the opportunity to continue their evolution. We must always remember that we are all children of God. There is only one difference, we are still living in the physical world while the leeches are living in the spirit world. Never take it upon yourself to deny a leech or anyone in the spirit world the opportunity to enter the light.

---

* Free-floater - A spirit who has freedom of movement and has not attached itself to anything or anyone.

** Holy Cross-see picture and explanation in Chap. 3.1

Chapter 1.10

HOW CAN I PROTECT MY NEWBORN FROM LEECH ATTACHMENTS?

I strongly recommend that you ask for God's blessing and protection for yourself and your baby several times during your pregnancy. Immediately after birth, bless your child in God's holy name and call upon the Blessed Virgin Mary for protection.

A newborn baby is most vulnerable during the first 24 months of life. Their newly formed energy field is still developing and has not yet hardened to protect the child on all levels (i.e. physical, spiritual).

At your earliest convenience, bless a small amount of oil (olive, castor, etc.) and anoint your newborn. Repeat God's holy name while rubbing a light coat of blessed oil on your newborn. This is a precautionary measure because at this present time in history we as human beings are inundated many times over with earthbound spirits. These spirits are unable to leave the planet because of their low consciousness. ***Do not be alarmed****. This information is intended to alert everyone about what is going on in the spiritual world in respect to addictive earthbound spirits.*

As a new mother, you receive a special gift from God, which is presented to you by the Blessed Mother. Through my guidance, I was given the message of the blessing that has been passed down from generation to generation. Mother Mary's message states: "Every mother that extends her hand in God's holy name to bless her child or any other child who is not of her bloodline, will be blessed and will carry and pass on this blessing for the next five generations."

If for some reason the new mother is unable to perform this blessing on her newborn baby, any family member or friend may ask for God's blessing for the newborn. It should be understood that this is only a temporary blessing until the mother is able to perform the blessing herself.

Chapter 1.11

SEX, TOBACCO, ALCOHOL AND DRUGS– HOW DO THESE ADDICTIONS AFFECT HUMANS?

I strongly believe that the following addictions: sex, tobacco, alcohol and drugs are the most dangerous addictions that any human can experience. All addictions are bad, but these four can literally destroy a human being's life and surroundings. Ironically, these same four addictions also affect an immense number of earthbound spirits. These spirits have a strong compulsive desire to continue to experience their former earthly cravings. These leeches attach themselves to a host body with the same addictions.

Their combined addictions create havoc when these earthbound spirits penetrate a person's spinal cord. The spinal cord has a concentration of energy, which allows for the strongest possible hold that any leech can have on a human.

There is another type of attachment that an addictive leech may have on a host body. This attachment is at the cellular level. In this level a leech can take total possession of the mental, physical, spiritual, and emotional bodies. I will not go into this material at this time. You will have to be taught the correct application for cellular leech removal in my workshop.

In my personal experience, the largest percentage of individuals trapped in these addictions are from ages 10 to 50 years. The symptoms displayed by these individuals include: suicide, severe sadness, disillusionment with life, and a deep threatening stare.

Chapter 1.12

CAN YOU HEAL YOUR OWN FAMILY?

Yes. However, I feel that this type of healing is somewhat limited because of the deep emotional attachment that family members have with one another. Experience has taught me that it is easier to give a friend or a stranger a healing. You are more likely to maintain balance and thus, work to your optimum level.

Trying to give a healing to your family is difficult because you become self-conscious about wanting to do your best, that you often lose the ability to simply let things flow. You may even become filled with doubt, which then allows negative thoughts and issues to arise, creating more inner turmoil. When these things occur, the healer's ability to perform diminishes.

In this situation I feel it is best to ask another healer for help. This gives you the opportunity to practice humility.

NOTES

UNCONDITIONAL LOVE

NOTES

___

___

___

___

___

___

___

UNCONDITIONAL LOVE

FORGIVE EVERYONE AND
BLESS EVERYONE WHO HURTS YOU
IN GOD'S HOLY NAME

CHAPTER TWO

Chapter 2

REASONS WHY YOUR SPIRIT LEAVES YOUR BODY

It has been my experience that the following examples cause your spirit to leave your body:

1. *Meditating Incorrectly*
2. *Accidents / Sudden Shock / Traumas (mental, physical, spiritual, and emotional)*
3. *Drugs*
4. *Not Closing Your Crown Chakra*
5. *Witchcraft (forces removal of client's spirit)*
6. *Severe Sadness*
7. *Not Wanting To Live*
8. *Leech Attachment*

In my workshops and meditations I teach and give you many explanations of how these occur.

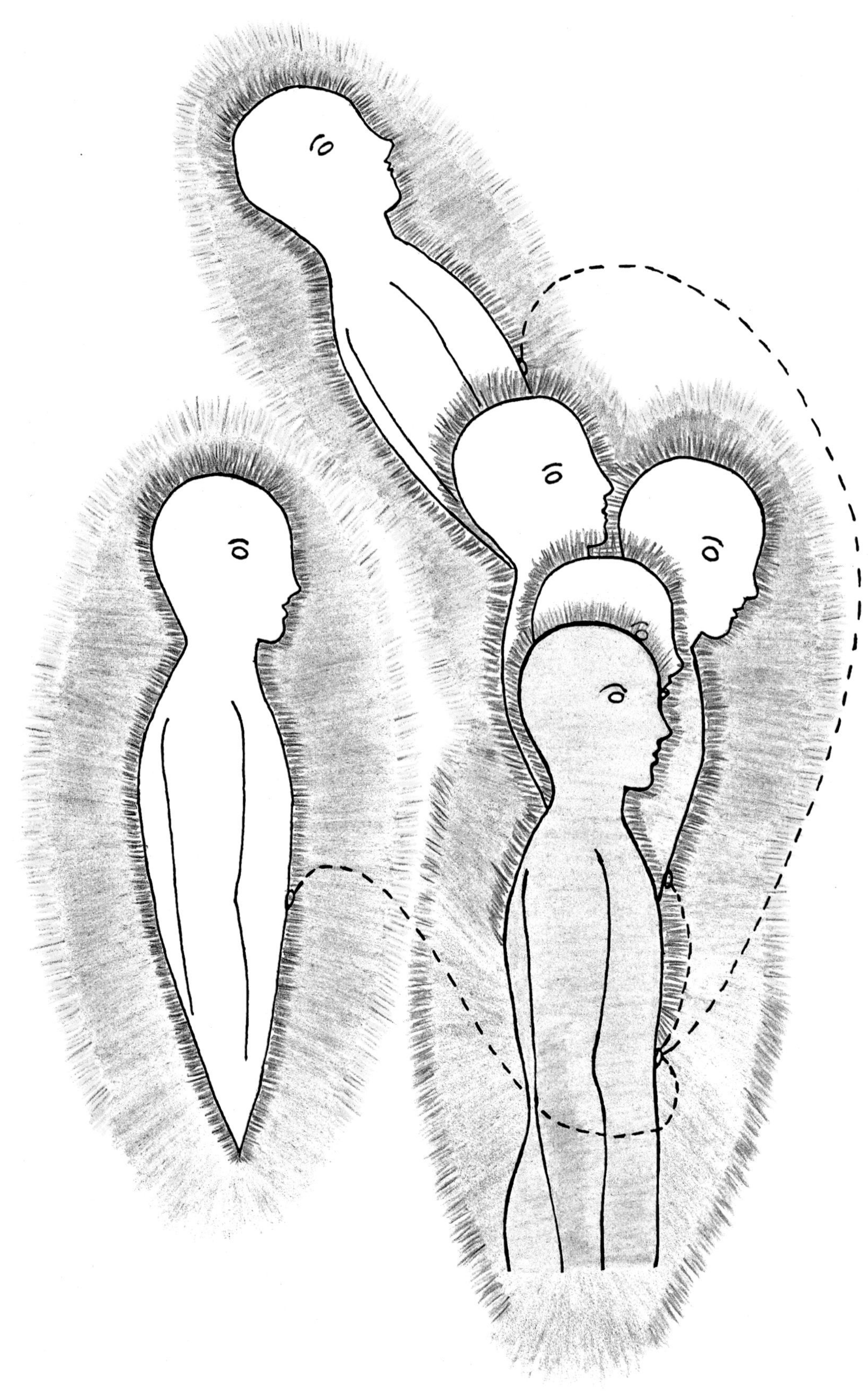

Chapter 2.1

SPIRIT OUT OF BODY SYMPTOMS

The most common symptoms are:

1. *Dizziness*
2. *Forgetfulness*
3. *Poor coordination, feeling off balance, tripping, clumsiness*
4. *Bad or disturbing dreams*
5. *Feeling out of balance while walking*
6. *Feeling off to one side*
7. *Feeling that the head is oversized*
8. *Glassy eyes, vacant look*
9. *Women will begin to have difficulty walking in high heels*
10. *Body feels numb*
11. *Psychic skills may increase*
12. *Unable to function in reality*
13. *Hard to concentrate or stay centered*
14. *Dislike yourself*

Individuals who experience most or all of these symptoms have a very difficult time living and functioning in reality. They need to have their spirits blessed and reinserted back into their body.

Chapter 2.2

MISINTERPRETING SPIRIT OUT OF BODY SYMPTOMS

If a person is spacey (spirit out of body) no traditional treatment will give permanent results. Many of my clients have sought various remedies for relief of their symptoms. These remedies include: herbal remedies, medical and mental health professionals, prescriptive drugs, alternative medicine, transfer of energy, acupuncture, kinesiology, massage therapy, etc. In most situations the client's symptoms have been misinterpreted. Their problem is spiritually based and requires a qualified spiritual healer with the gift of spirit insertion.

The moment that the spirit is inserted back into the individual's body, they report many of the following sensations: tingling, a sudden rush of energy, an emotional release of happiness, and a feeling of fullness within.

All the "Spirit out of Body" symptoms previously mentioned are removed immediately. At the moment of spirit insertion the healing is felt within the center of the person's being. They are lost for words and only the joy and sparkle in their eyes tells you everything.

Chapter 2.3

INDIVIDUALS REQUIRING SPIRIT INSERTION IS GROWING

During my many years of spiritual healing I have encountered a growing number of clients who have their spirits out of their bodies. Spirit out of body means that the spirit/soul has shifted or moved out of the physical body.** This situation leaves the person with little or no will power and unable to function in reality. People are most vulnerable to leech attachment at this time.*

Approximately 85% of individuals who attend my workshops, meditations, and healings require a spirit insertion healing.

---

* Spirit/soul are considered one and the same.

** See illustration on p. 62

Chapter 2.4

CAN MY SPIRIT BE REINSERTED INTO MY PHYSICAL BODY?

Yes, your spirit can be reinserted into your physical body thus restoring it to perfect balance and harmony.

First, you should check the Spirit Out of Body Symptoms Chart (See Chap. 2.1). If you are experiencing most or all of the symptoms, there is a good possibility that your problems are spiritually based.

I would like to give you a better understanding of how you should feel after your spirit has been reinserted. You should feel as though you are on a "natural high." You should also experience a sense of well-being in all areas of your life.

If these feelings are not experienced immediately or within a few days, I would question whether the spirit insertion was done correctly or even done at all.

However, if after your spirit insertion healing has been successfully completed, and the symptoms persist without any relief it is not spiritually based. My advice to you would be to seek medical or psychological evaluations for proper treatment.

Chapter 2.5

CAN ALL HEALERS DO SPIRIT INSERTION?

No, not all spiritual healers can do spirit insertion. ***Spirit insertion is a gift from God.*** *Do not assume that all spiritual healers have this gift. This gift is given to your spirit guide to be shared with you, the healer, and to be used in the physical world to help humanity.*

I have been blessed to witness many spontaneous healings after spirit insertion. This healing can be done within a few minutes by a qualified healer. A tremendous feeling of well-being is felt by many of my clients. The value of such a healing is priceless. Symptoms previously experienced suddenly disappear.

All levels are balanced simultaneously as spirit insertion takes place. However, some clients who process mentally, may have a delayed reaction. They're waiting for something to happen when it has already occurred.

Warning to Clients: *It has been my personal experience that too many times clients have come in complaining about the outrageous amount of money they have spent on a healing. Some pay hundreds, even thousands of dollars for a healing and either the healing was started and never completed or nothing was done at all. This leaves the client frustrated, upset, and they lose faith in all healers.*

For the sake of integrity and the protection of the client, a complete spiritual healing should not exceed $200.00 (two hundred U.S. dollars). A reasonable time of 1-2 hours should be allowed for this type of session. This is not "carved in stone," it is just to bring awareness to the general public. Please use common sense.*

---

* A complete spiritual healing should consist of: removal of all negative energies, witchcraft, leech removal, spirit insertion, cleansing, balancing, and a blessing.

Chapter 2.6

SEQUENCE OF HEALINGS

I recommend that three healings be given in this order. The first healing should be on the spiritual level. **Always allow 30 days before another healing session.** *Thirty days is recommended to let the first healing take its course and to determine what else is needed. The second healing I recommend should be on the emotional level. This healing consists of opening your heart, forgiving yourself, asking for God's forgiveness, and releasing patterns that have kept you in denial. This healing is basically a cleansing session. The last healing,* ***if needed****, should be done on the physical level (i.e. faith healing, massage healing, herbal remedies, etc.).*

The reason I give the healings in this order can best be compared to a client going to a physician, and the doctor determines that three major surgeries are needed: leg amputation, liver, and kidney transplants. Obviously, all these surgeries cannot be performed in one day.

Chapter 2.7

TESTIMONIAL

	June 1999, Perth, Australia
Name:	Mary, 34 years of age
Diagnosis:	Spirit Out of Body
Treatment:	Reinsertion of Spirit
Results:	Mary experienced sensations in her legs for the first time in thirty years. She noticed that she felt taller and that her legs felt heavy. This is known as "grounding the individual" to Mother Earth. She started running and doing cartwheels...something she had never been able to do.

When Mary went home that evening she shared her newfound joy with others. Due to spirit insertion Mary now had the strength to trigger old memories from her subconscious mind. These memories brought her back to the age of four when she was sexually molested. As the memories flooded her mind, she became overwhelmed and was unable to face the reality of that experience, so her spirit left her physical body once again. The next day she returned feeling unhappy. I had to reinsert her spirit, tie it in, and close her crown chakra to prevent the same problem from reoccurring.

Painful experiences such as molestation will generally cause your spirit to leave your physical body. This happens because returning to your physical body means that you need to address those traumas, hurts, or issues that caused your spirit to leave your body in the first place.

For individuals who have sustained such traumas, it is safer to stay in denial than to acknowledge and face the truth and live in reality. These individuals who have not addressed and released their painful memories have created blockages in all levels within their conscious and subconscious minds.

In cases like Mary's, the client may require further treatment on all levels, depending on their evolution and strength of spirit. Further treatment will depend on whether they can cope with reality or not.

There is another situation that I would like to point out because of its similarity to Mary's case. This case involves individuals who have been in a relationship while their spirit has been out of their bodies for most of their lives. When spirit insertion takes place, these individuals will find it extremely difficult to understand and accept that they do not really know their partner. Their relationship has been a superficial relationship based upon denial rather than living the truth.

In both of these situations, I recommend that the clients seek further treatment. I suggest the following self-treatments:

1. *Pray to God for support and healing.*
2. *Surrender yourself to God.*
3. *Accept and Love yourself.*
4. *Do not punish yourself.*
5. *Take time to meditate.*
6. *Be positive in all your thoughts.*
7. *Keep yourself busy and productive.*
8. *Remember you have Freedom of Choice.*

I also suggest the following professional treatments:

1. *Psychiatrist or Psychologist with spiritual awareness and consciousness*
2. *Spiritual support group or counseling sessions*
3. *Kinesiologist, certified homeopath or naturopath*

NOTES

UNCONDITIONAL LOVE

LOVE YOURSELF AND FORGIVE YOURSELF

CHAPTER THREE

Chapter 3

ARE YOU FREE OF LEECHES? (SELF-TEST)

The following is a method that I have developed to test yourself for leeches. My test will determine whether or not you have a leech. Using this method will insure your integrity. You will also be able to perceive or use your intuition without any negative influences or distortions. In addition, you will be practicing good healer-hygiene techniques, which will keep you and your client safe.

This test must be done one (1) to two (2) days before a healing. *You should also be preparing yourself by praying, having a good attitude and remaining balanced.*

Self-Test

1. *Mirror*
2. *Take towel, place sprig of rue with blessed olive oil on it.*
3. *Clean mirror entirely with olive oil and rue solution.*
4. *Clean mirror with rubbing alcohol (clean towel).*
5. *Stand 3 feet from mirror.*
6. *Bless mirror—"I bless you in the name of God."*

7. *Bent-arm position with palms toward mirror*

8. *Maintain constant eye contact with mirror image while verbally blessing your image in God's holy name.*

9. *Slowly move forward towards mirror, one step at a time, and continue verbally blessing your image. Constant eye contact must be maintained throughout the entire test.*

10. *To detect a leech, look for:*
    a. *a piercing stare*
    b. *a feeling of fear*
    c. *a cold feeling causing **bad** goose bumps*
    d. *twitching or facial distortions*
    e. *a feeling of dislike for yourself*

11. *If **NO LEECH** — Nothing will be felt.*

Client's Test

1. *Stand 5 feet from client.*

2. *Bless client—"I bless you in the name of God."*

3. *Bent-arm position with palms toward client*

4. *Healer and client must maintain constant eye contact while healer slowly moves toward client. (Healer must give unconditional love throughout entire Leech Test.)*

5. *Look for signs given in Self-Test, step 10.*

UNCONDITIONAL LOVE

BLESSING OF THE CROSS

Anyone who has faith in God may bless the cross. Not all blessings are equal in spiritual strength. Therefore, the cross will only work on the strength of the blessing it receives. I have been blessed by the Holy Spirit to give blessings. If you wish, I will bless your cross. Send a photograph and I will present your cross to God. ***After the blessing, the Holy Cross has the spiritual strength to assist you.***

HOLY CROSS ON/OFF PROCEDURES

1. *Light the tea candles on the Holy Cross.*
2. *Begin your opening prayer.*
3. *State your intent.*
   Examples:
   - *Leech Removal*
   - *Open Your (Emotional) Heart*
   - *Soul Attunement*
   - *Personal Healing*
   - *Healings for others*
4. *The Holy Cross is now* ***spiritually*** *activated and ready to assist and work with you.*
5. *At the end of your session, close down the activation of the Holy Cross with your intent.*
6. *The Holy Cross should not be left on spiritually because it will still be working without supervision. This is not a good spiritual healer-hygiene practice.*

Chapter 3.1

PREPARING FOR LEECH REMOVAL

1. *Prepare Holy Cross by lighting all seven tea light candles.*

2. *Pray for God's blessing, protection, and guidance before commencing any work.*

3. ***Blessed** belt, headband, wrist and ankle bands, rue, olive oil and lemon drink.* Charcoal and frankincense used for smudging. Blessed cutting stone is used for all spiritual incisions.*

* 1 T Olive Oil with 1/2 freshly squeezed lemon

BLESSED BELT AND HEAD BAND GIVES YOU MORE SPIRITUAL STRENGTH AND PROTECTION

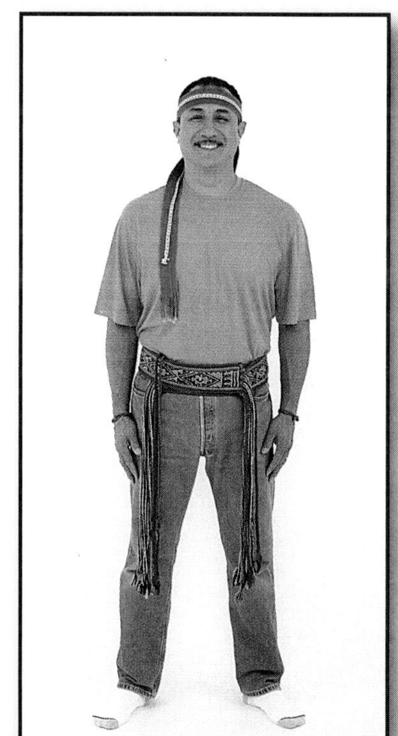

4. *Preparing the Triangles.*

(a) *Masking tape will be used to prepare all triangles.*
(b) *Prepare the first triangle 3' away from the Holy Cross, having 3 equal sides, 2' in length.*
(c) *Second triangle is placed 4' from the first triangle having 3 equal sides, 5' in length.**

* Everything can be adjusted according to your space or needs.

5. *Smudge entire work area with incense (frankincense).*

6. *Ask God to please bless and activate both triangles and Holy Cross.*

The Triangle is a very important symbol.
It represents God's presence.

GOD
THE FATHER

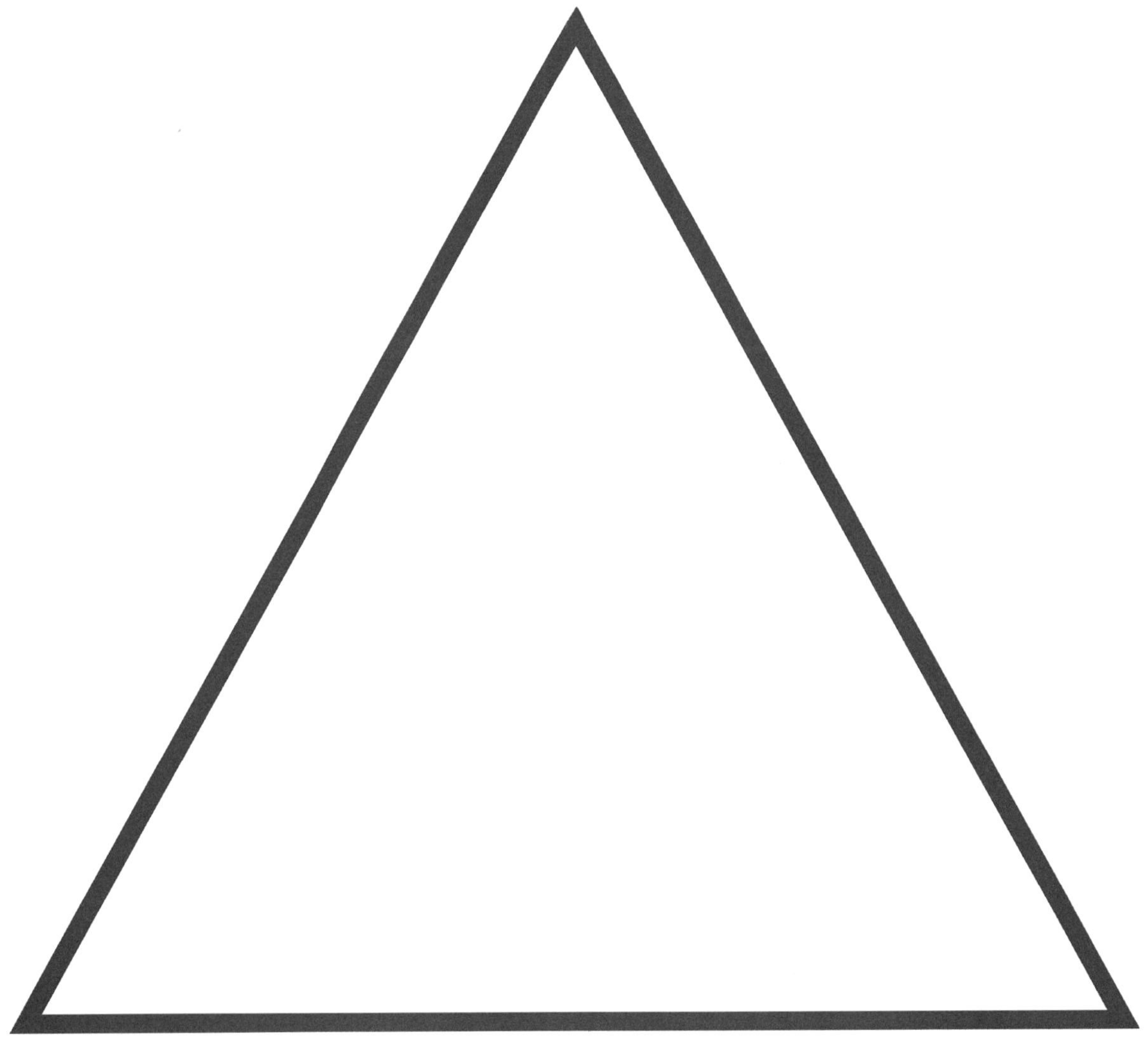

GOD
THE SON

GOD
THE HOLY SPIRIT

The individuals who choose to participate must have faith in God, a clean mind, and have unconditional love for humanity.

7. *Your position within the triangle will be determined by which corner you feel pulled towards.*

8. *One person will stand within each point of the triangle. All will face the host body.*

9. ***Everyone's position is a number one position.***

10. ***All** positions will be determined by where you are pulled. If you don't feel pulled towards a position in the work area, your job is to pray. Within the group everyone is praying. Some may be called to substitute.*

11. *It is imperative that you tune in and listen to your heart. **NO TIME FOR EGO.** This has to be **a team effort**.*

12. *God the Father position (top of triangle) will send unconditional love and light to the spine of the host body to allow the spine to open and release trapped earthbound spirits.*

13. *The individuals taking God the Son and God the Holy Spirit positions will send unconditional love and light to the host body's aura/energy field.*

14. *The two (2) holders (4th and 5th positions) are there to support the client's physical body. Always be focused and alert.*

Entire Leech Removal Set-Up

4th, 5th, & 6th Positions

15. *Both wrists of the host body must be held to ensure the client's safety.*

16. *The two (2) holders (4th & 5th positions) should* ***never*** *close their eyes. They should be aware of what is going on and lend their support to the host body.*

17. *The holders must wear green and red ribbons on both wrists and ankles for spiritual protection.*

18. *If the holders have a blessed belt, they should wear it for grounding, protection, and spiritual strength.*

19. *Floater/leader (6th position) carries a big responsibility. The floater/leader is responsible for removing the leeches.*

20. *The floater/leader (6th position) must always be alert and in constant communication with all healers, client, and earthbound spirits. He must gain the trust of the earthbound spirits in order to do the leech removal. The floater must also ensure that all participants are synchronized.*

21. *Any additional healers must be prepared to assume any position as the need arises. Additionally, they must remain in constant prayer because prayer gives spiritual strength and protection to all involved.*

Chapter 3.2

LEECH REMOVAL TECHNIQUES

Warm-Up/Melt Down

1. *God the Father position sends unconditional love and light to entire spine area.*
2. *God the Son and God the Holy Spirit positions send unconditional love and light to entire aura/energy field.*
3. *All triangle participants **must** keep their eyes closed.*
4. *Approximately 5 minutes are needed to create a warm-up/meltdown effect.*
5. *Meltdown effect loosens leeches allowing them to move freely within the energy field.*
6. *As a reminder — Everyone **must** be honest with themselves while giving unconditional love, otherwise, meltdown will not occur.*
7. *During the meltdown period, floater should be asking the client whether he is feeling any pain or discomfort.*
8. *Floater must also be communicating with the earthbound spirit in a **non-threatening manner** during the meltdown period.*
9. *Floater must speak loudly enough so the entire group knows what's going on.*
10. *Holders must remain in constant visual contact with the host body and be ready for any reaction as they support the physical body.*
11. *It is imperative that the client resonates with self-love while forgiving the leeches and everyone who has ever hurt him.*

12. *Floater begins by asking the earthbound spirit if it wishes to enter the Holy Cross of light and receive God's blessing.*
13. *Some leeches wish to go to the light but will require help in being released because they are entangled within the energy field.*
14. *The Holy Cross acts like a huge vacuum.* ***DO NOT STAND*** *between your client and the Holy Cross.*
15. *Floater is now ready to enter his position and remove the earthbound spirit from the host body.*

Leech Removal from Upper Body

Press and pull is done in one continuous sweep. Hands must ***never*** *leave the client's body until you toss the leech into the Holy Cross.*

Left Side of Body:

Shoulder-hand position

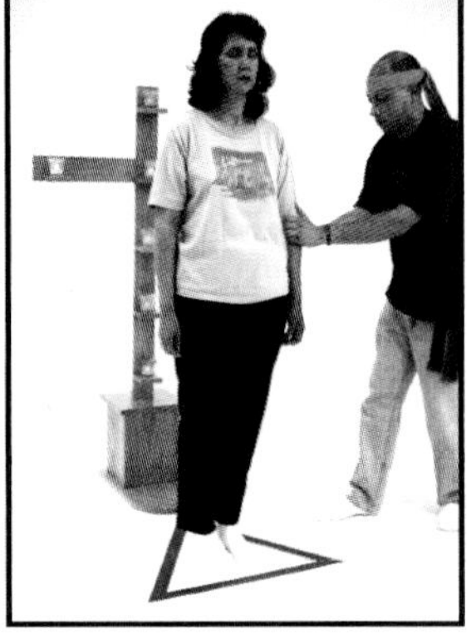

From shoulder to elbow

From elbow off hand

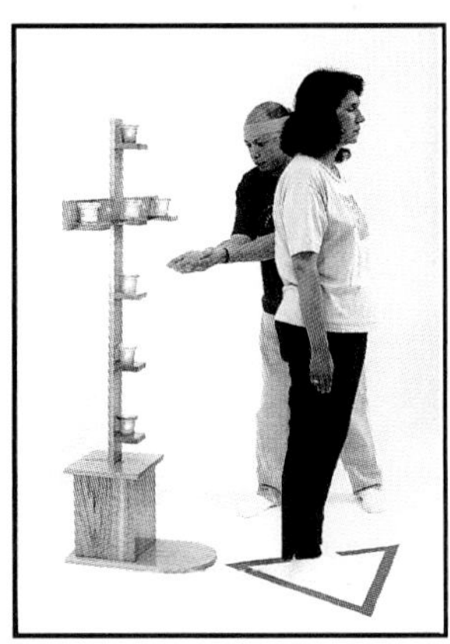

Toss into Holy Cross

Right Side of Body:

Shoulder-hand position

From shoulder to elbow

From elbow off hand

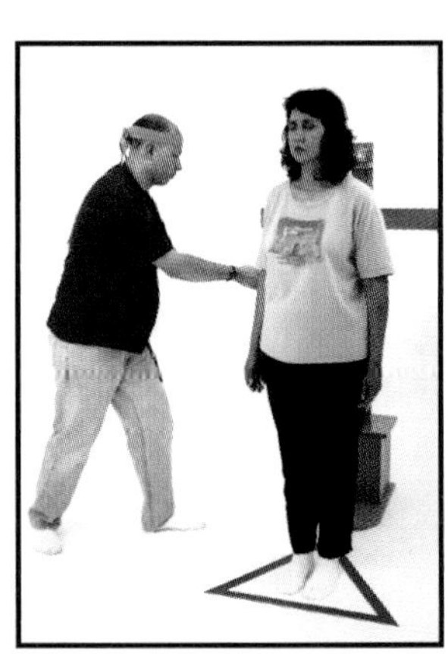

Toss into Holy Cross

Leech Removal from Lower Body

*Press and pull is done in one continuous sweep. Hands must **never** leave the client's body until you toss the leech into the Holy Cross.*

Left Side of Body:

Hand positions on the waist

Press and pull from waist to knee

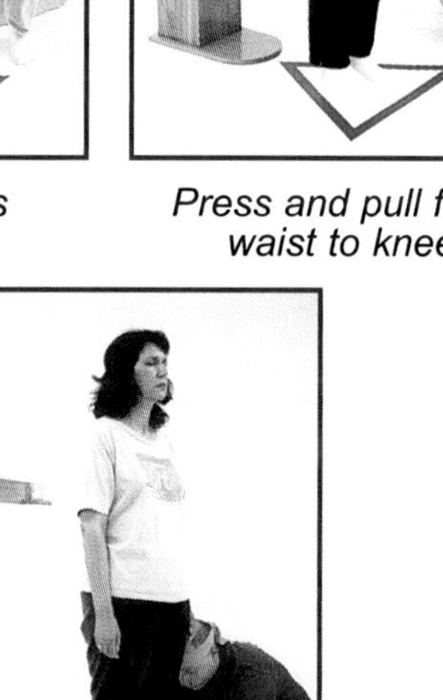

Press and pull from knee to ankle

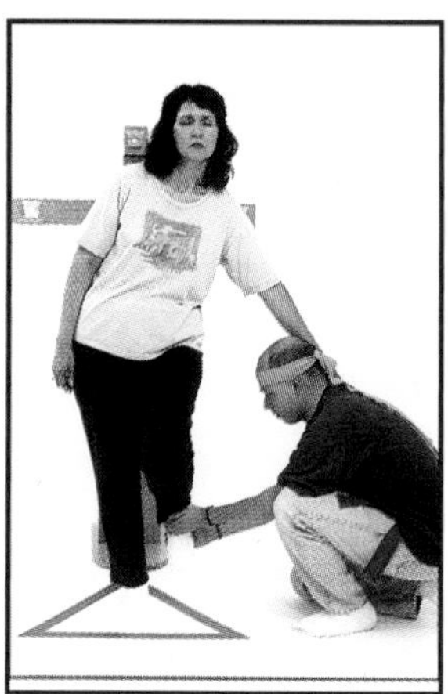

Clean bottom of foot

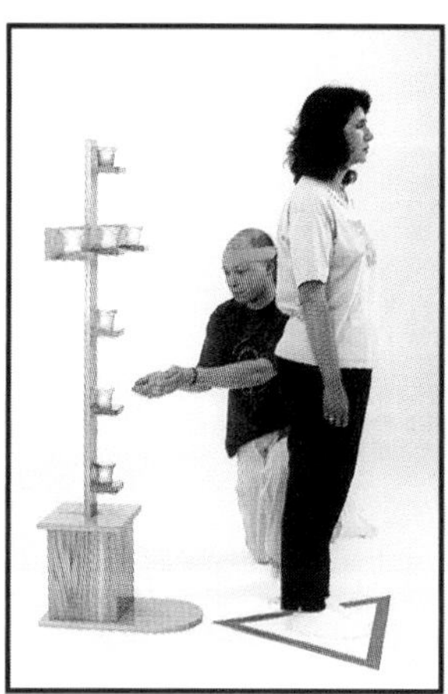

Toss into Holy Cross

Right Side of Body:

Hand positions on the waist

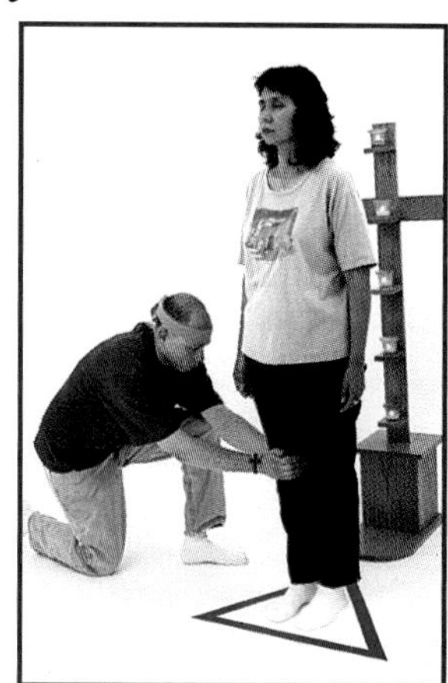

Press and pull from waist to knee

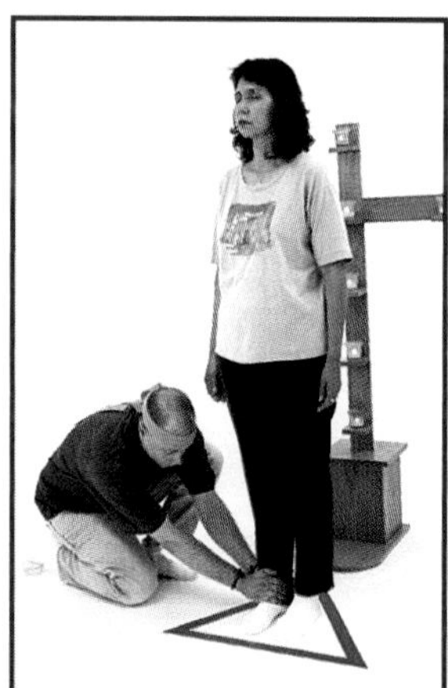

Press and pull from knee to ankle

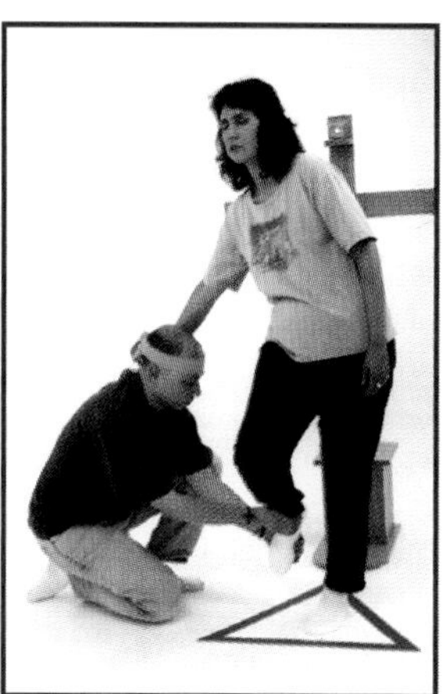

Clean bottom of foot

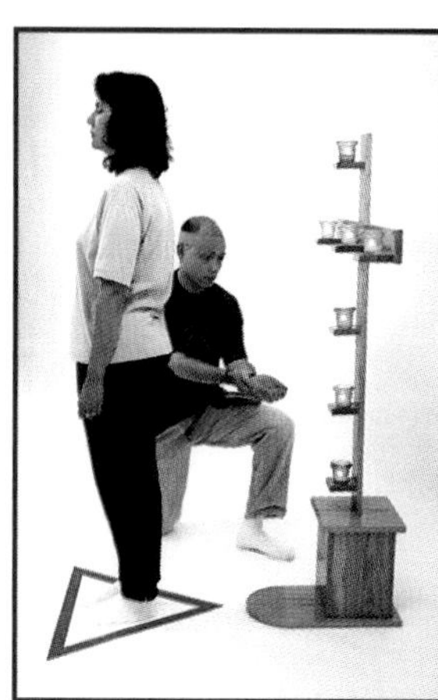

Toss into Holy Cross

16. Other important areas where leeches attach themselves are the head and spinal areas. It is critical that the floater clears these areas precisely as illustrated.

Leech Removal from Head and Spine Areas

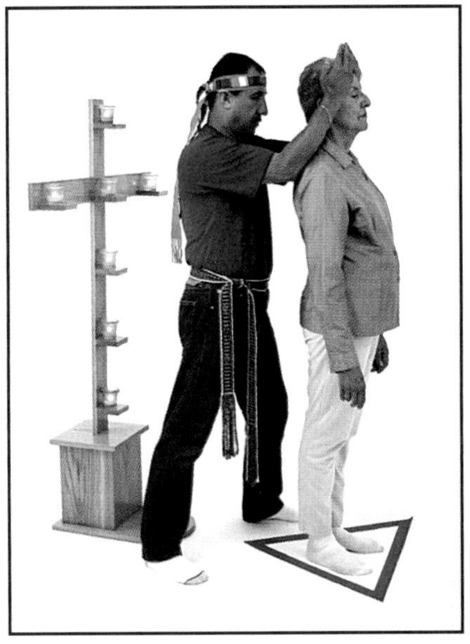

Head-hand position

Pull down to shoulders

Pull downwards to waist

Pass tailbone

Toss to Holy Cross

17. *If, while the floater is using his intuition and doubt arises,* ***NEVER GUESS*** *where the host body is experiencing any pain or discomfort.* ***ASK THE CLIENT.***

18. *Once the client has responded, the floater will go directly to that spot. Floater will pull and remove the leech that is causing the pain or discomfort.*

19. *Pain and discomfort in different parts of the body may be due to leech movement.*

CAUTION: If the pain persists, ask the client if they have had pain there previously or if it just occurred during the healing. This is to distinguish between a pre-existing injury/condition or pain caused by a leech.

20. *Make sure you check the nape area. This is a spiritual door/opening where earthbound spirits can hide and cause severe neck and shoulder pain. You must remove all intruders within this area.*

Leech Removal Within the Nape:

From the side, place one hand on client's forehead. This ensures a good hand position to remove any leech within the nape. Use your inner guidance to feel and sense the leech.

When ready, ask God to intercede on your behalf. When you feel God's presence, pull the leech from the nape.

Toss the leech into the Holy Cross.

21. *These techniques usually work for most earthbound spirits because not all spirits are evil, just addictive.*

22. *If the leech removal does not work, either the healers were not in sync or their sincerity was not present. Therefore, the spiritual strength was not available to remove the leeches.*

23. *If you decide to try again,* ***UNDERSTAND THAT YOU ONLY HAVE ONE MORE ATTEMPT****. More attempts would be too physically and emotionally draining for all involved.*

NOTES

UNCONDITIONAL LOVE

Chapter 3.3

LEECH ATTACHMENTS WITHIN THE CHAKRAS

Chakra leech attachments are not always obvious. We must always be aware and check all of the client's main chakras. Many times I have encountered leeches lodged deeply within the solar plexus or heart chakra.

This sort of attachment is apparent if after the removal of earthbound spirits, the client still feels pain. This is especially true if the pain is close to any of the main chakras. All main chakras are vulnerable to leech attachments.

The procedure for removing a leech from a chakra is more intense than that of the physical body and energy field. *(See pg. 98)*

Do not underestimate the ability of a leech. It can move from one chakra to another. If you are not intuitive enough, ***do not guess*** *where the leech has gone. A great deal of the time, the client is aware of the pain and direction the leech is traveling.* ***Ask your client for guidance when you are unsure.***

No one knows it all. *Unconditional love, faith, and compassion are the main elements needed to accomplish leech removal from the chakras.*

Remember: As a team, we can work together for the betterment of humanity.

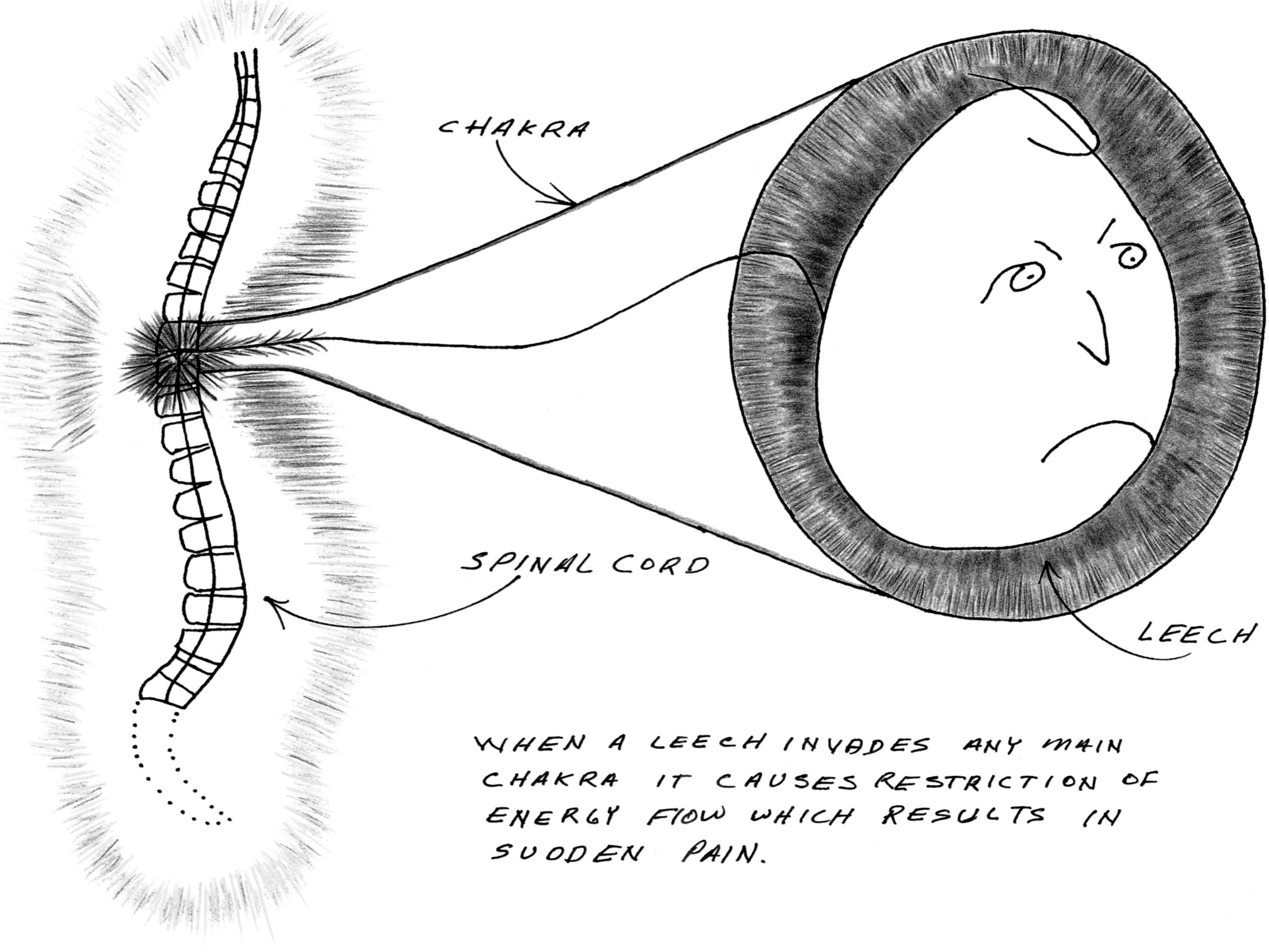
CHAKRA
SPINAL CORD
LEECH
WHEN A LEECH INVADES ANY MAIN
CHAKRA IT CAUSES RESTRICTION OF
ENERGY FLOW WHICH RESULTS IN
SUDDEN PAIN.

Chapter 3.4

EXTRACTING LEECHES FROM CHAKRAS

1. *The Holy Cross is needed (See p. 79).*

2. *The Holy Cross healings are done by a team of six healers (minimum).*

3. *A team of 10 healers is preferable.*

4. *All group members drink a lemon juice and olive oil mixture. (1/2 lemon and 1T olive oil) Ask God to bless this mixture before drinking.*

5. *Place rue (wrapped in tissue) over the third eye area under your headband for protection.*

6. *Every team member must wear red and green ribbons or bands around his wrists and ankles for protection.*

7. *Give client blessed lemon and olive oil drink.*

8. *The client's back must **always** face the Holy Cross. This position is best for everyone involved as it aids the healer in removing the leeches* and provides less discomfort to the client.*

9. *Leech Extractor — prepare your heart to give total unconditional love to humanity. With complete sincerity ask God's permission to allow your hand to be the Hand of Christ.*

10. *Now, extractor steps into position in front of the client to remove the leech.*

11. *When you feel the Hand of God, move towards the chakra. You will see the leech's face or feel and sense its presence. With all God's Love and Compassion, go into the chakra (tunnel) in search of the leech. The leech will sense your intent and will then try to move into the spinal cord where it will have freedom of movement. Also, be aware that if your first attempt is unsuccessful, the leech may break apart, thus making the task harder for all involved.***

* **Leeches** are not to be confused with dirty energy (trauma) or negative thought forms and emotions.
Leeches are individuals who have passed over into the spirit world. They are addicted earthbound spirits who are drawn to you by your negative attitude and emotions.

** **I want to caution you that repeated attempts may cause discomfort within the general area of the chakra you are working on.**

12. *Take hold of the leech and pull it straight out and then toss the leech into the Holy Cross. Immediately afterwards, cut-off by striking your hands. It is imperative that you always cut-off energetically from the client.*

13. *If the Extractor is fearful, the leech will take this fear and empower itself and then challenge the Extractor. This is why it is so important to remain with total unconditional love throughout the entire removal procedure.*

14. *While the Extractor is doing the removal, the others in the triangle are sending unconditional love and light to their designated areas. (See p. 87)*

15. *Have a bucket ready as the client may throw up. If he does, help him bring it up by sliding your hand gently up his spine.*

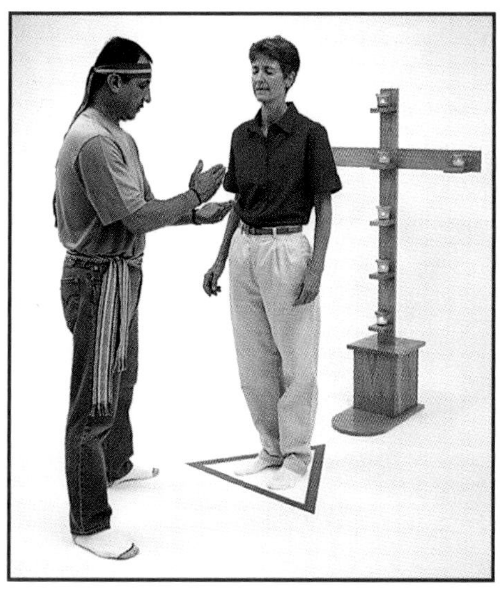

16. *Ask the client how he feels.*

17. *Use common sense when your client describes something moving in his body. For example, "Does it feel good or bad?" He may be feeling a release and his once stagnated energy is now moving freely throughout his body.*

18. *Leech removal can be done by one (1) person who is spiritually gifted and carries the spiritual strength within his heart and soul. He must have faith, integrity, unconditional love, acceptance of God, and communion with God.* ***This gift is entrusted to the healer by God.*** *Spiritual guides of high frequency who are of God's consciousness will help the healer share this gift with humanity.*

19. *In this present time of consciousness, these individual healers are few and far between.*

20. *I cannot emphasize enough the importance of* ***teamwork****. Teamwork helps build spiritual strength and confidence, which leads to faith.*

In many of my workshops and meditations I have repeatedly tried to teach unity among all new and experienced healers. When we humbly respect others for their gifts, we in turn are respected for who we are and our gifts are also acknowledged.

It has come to my consciousness that other techniques are currently being used. I do not pretend or claim that my method is the only method. However, I can safely say that I feel it is one of the best natural methods available. We learn, grow in consciousness, and create good karma when assisting lost souls into the path of light. This is a very good feeling.

NOTES

UNCONDITIONAL LOVE

Chapter 3.5

INDIVIDUAL SPIRIT INSERTION

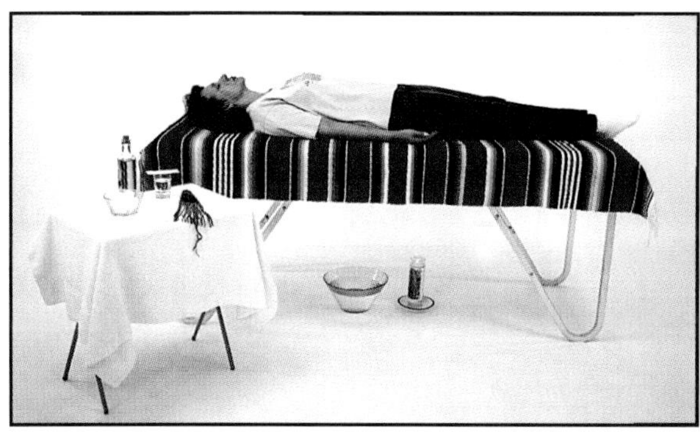

1. *Client on table, uncrossed legs, palms up*

2. *Blessed clear glass of water (represents River Jordan) containing client's full birth name on a piece of paper.*

3. *Put blessed olive oil on client's head (crown area) for ease of entry of his spirit.*

4. *Make a spiritual incision with cutting stone from front to back of head while saying, "God the Father, God the Son, God the Holy Spirit".*

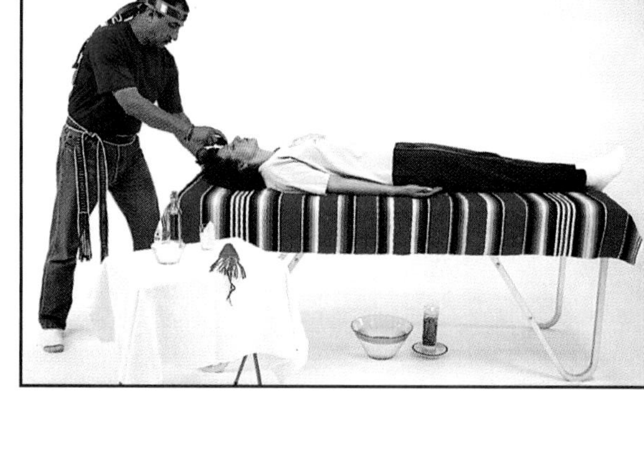

5. *Blessing for Spirit Insertion—say, "Divine Father, please hear my petition to bless your child and to reinsert his spirit".*

6. *Wait for God's answer.*

7. *Client's spirit is placed in a glass of water.*

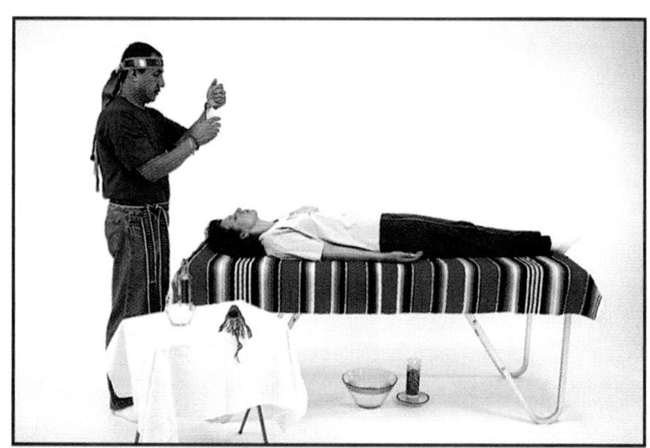

8. *Healer now recites the following prayer:*

Divine Father,
I present to you your child. I ask you, Father, to receive and redress your child with loving arms. I ask that you baptize your child with the sacred waters of the River Jordan. I also ask that your child be reawakened to your truth, light, and knowing of your Divine presence. You are God the Father and this is your child. I implore you, Father, that your child receive all that is of your Divine will. I ask that your child remember your Holy Name and that You are omnipotent, and that You are unconditional love and compassion. You are infinite — You are God.

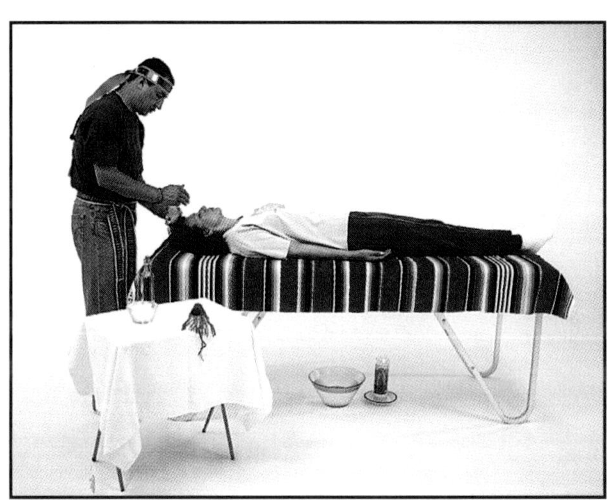

9. *Drip water from the River Jordan on the client's forehead.*

10. *Your spirit guide and you will wait until God hands you His child's spirit, and at that moment you will feel the truth in your heart. (Example: I receive the spirit in the form of a little baby. Sometimes, the spirit is accompanied by the Holy Spirit, the Holy Cross or Jesus Christ. Then I know I am ready to insert the spirit back into the body.)*

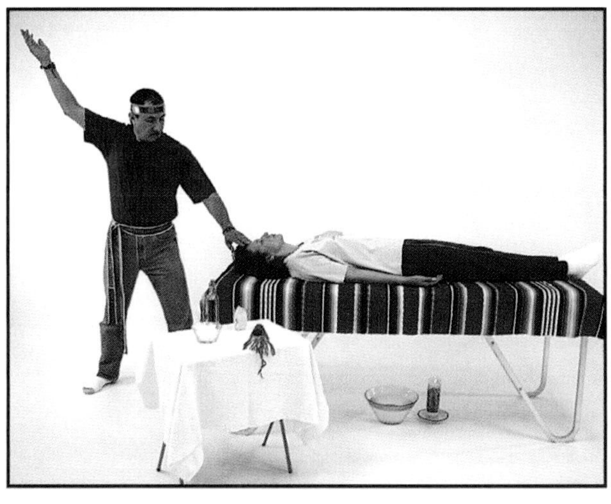

11. *Place your left hand on client's forehead while holding their spirit above your head in your right hand.*

12. *Begin circling your hand above your head to gain momentum for insertion.*

13. *Continue circling while you and your client say out loud:*

Healer:	"IN THE NAME OF GOD THE FATHER."
Client:	"(FULL BIRTH NAME), I AM HERE."
Healer:	"IN THE NAME OF GOD THE SON."
Client:	"(FULL BIRTH NAME), I AM HERE."
Healer:	"IN THE NAME OF GOD THE HOLY SPIRIT."
Client:	"(FULL BIRTH NAME), I AM HERE."

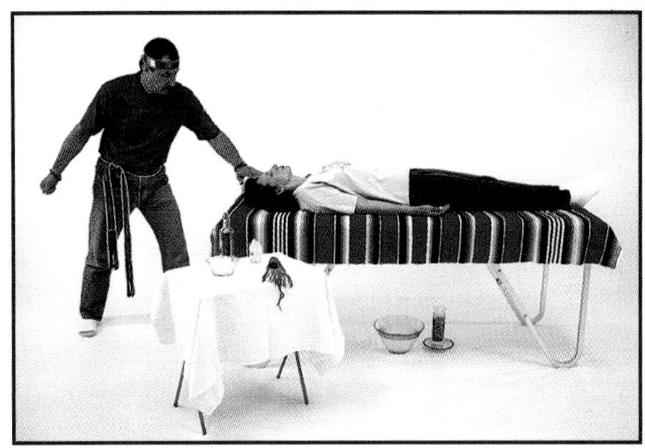

14. *Just before insertion, throw your arm back (as if delivering a softball pitch).*

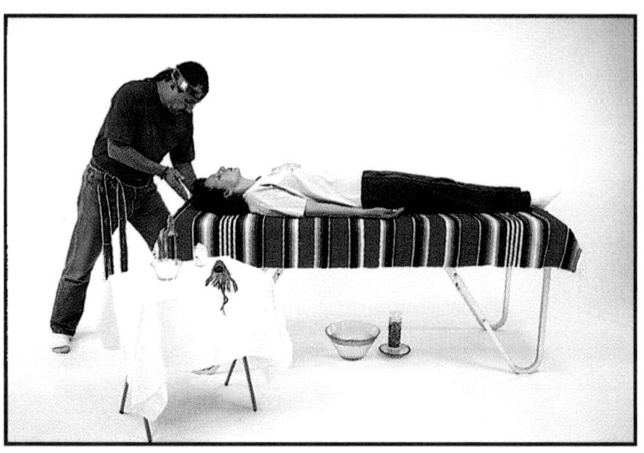

15. *Forcefully push the spirit into his crown and down to his feet.*

This procedure is not intended to harm the physical body. Remember, the insertion is being done with spiritual strength — Not physical force.

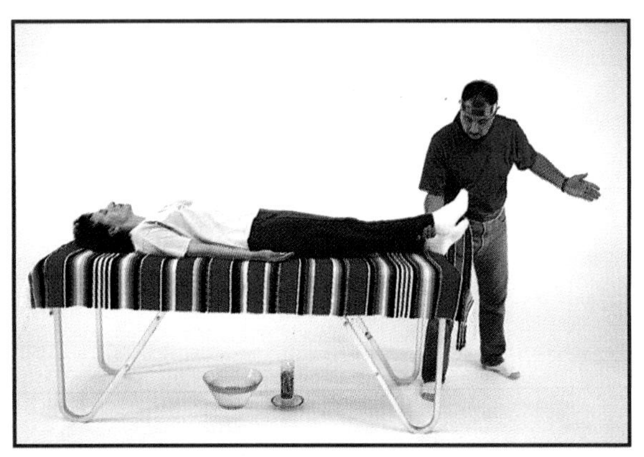

16. *Go to client's feet and slap his soles with a strong slap (without causing pain). This is to awaken his spirit. Ask client to breathe deeply once or twice.*

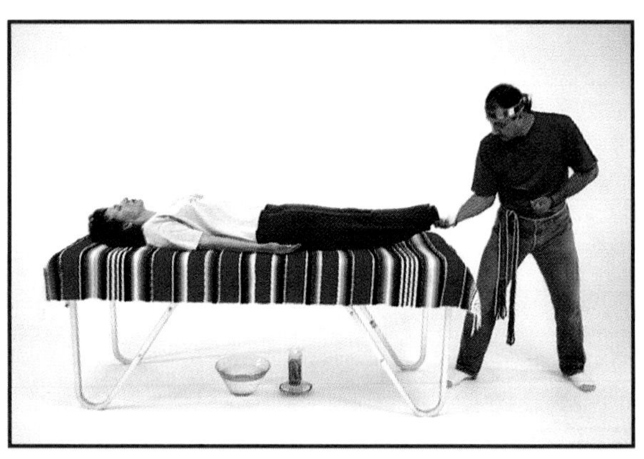

17. *Pull the spirit through feet.*

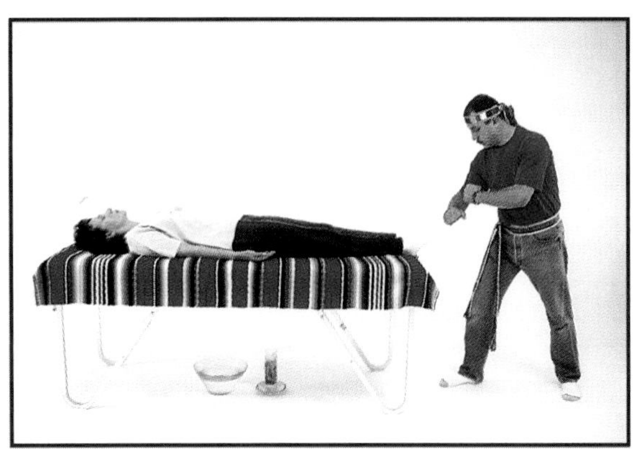

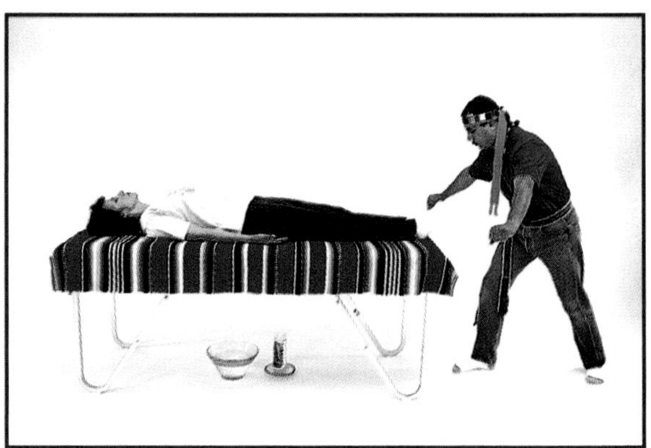

18. *Tie to the physical body. Now you are ready to move into the next procedure.* *(See next page)*

Bring to "Present Time of Consciousness."
(Steps "a" through "i")

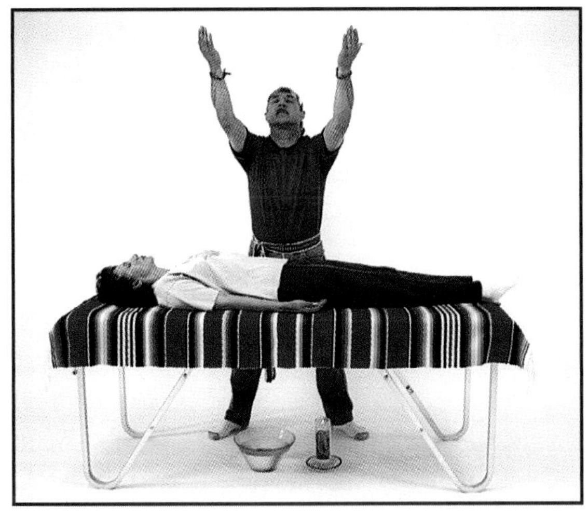

a. Stand above the client at midsection with hands open above your head.

b. Ask God's permission and blessing for the client.

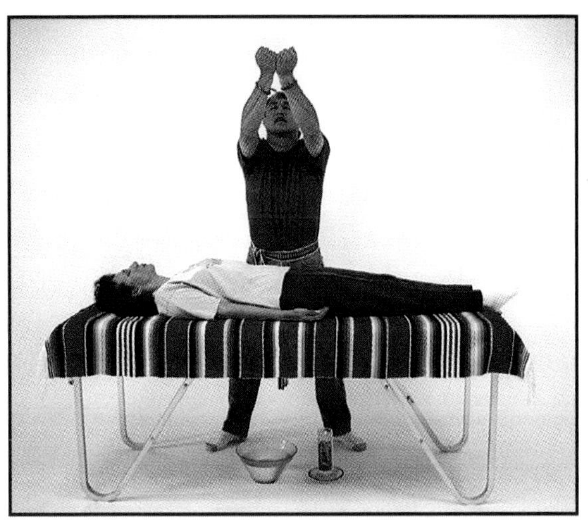

c. When you feel God's blessing close your fists.

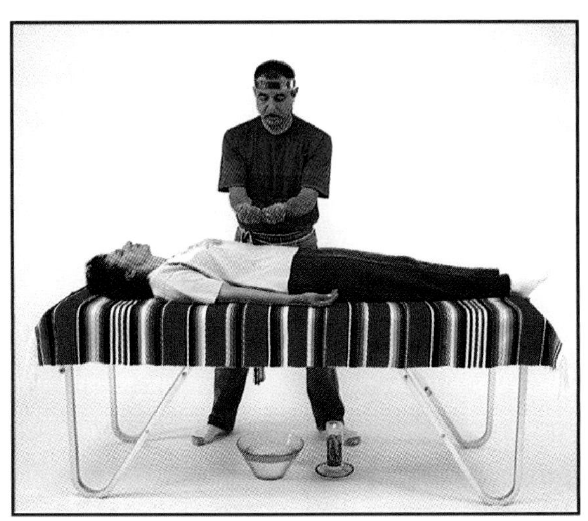

d. Bring closed fists down (close together) to just above client's navel.

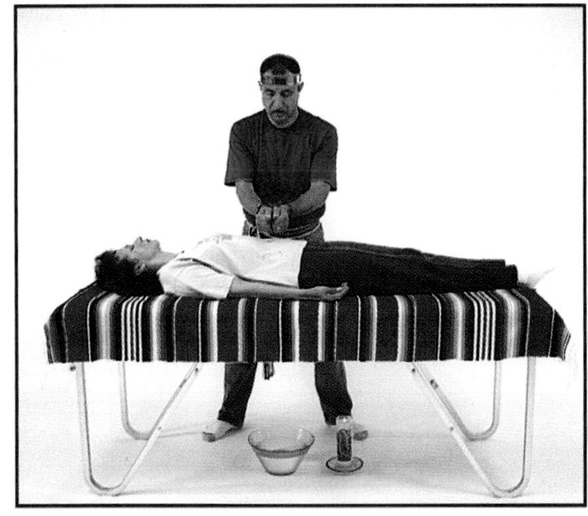

e. Rotate fists inward, fingers to fingers.

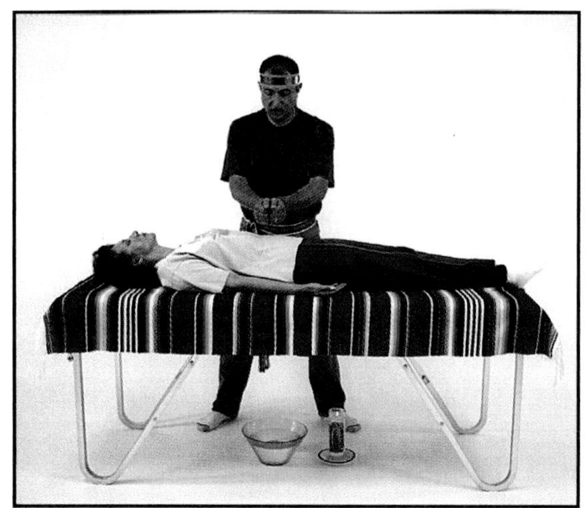

f. *Raise fists up 2-3 inches.*

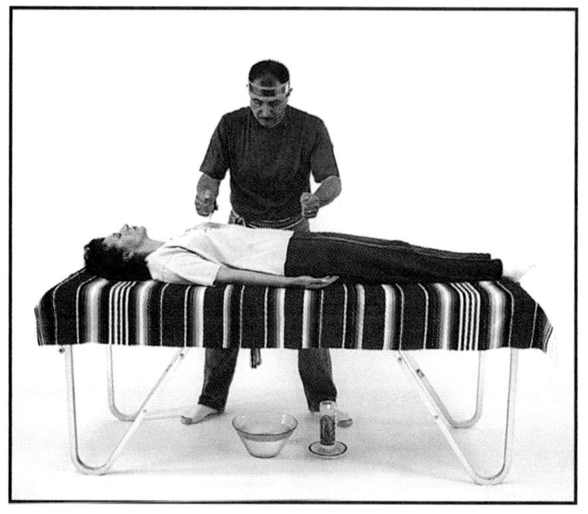

g. *Separate arms with fisted hands (approximately 12 inches).*

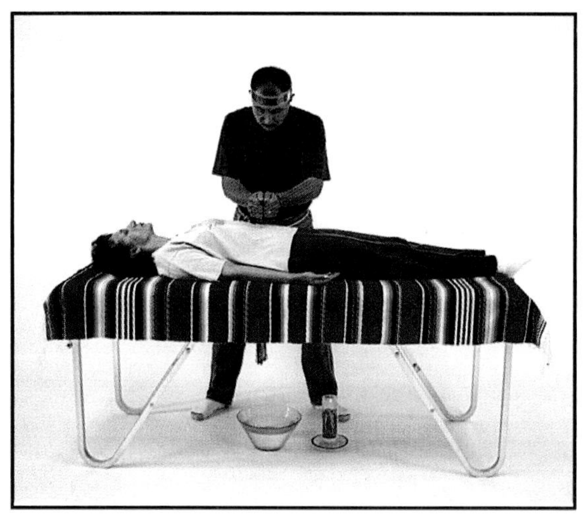

h. *Quickly bring fisted hands together.*

i. *Then immediately extend to healer's full arm extension and finish with palms open and facing downward.*

19. *Balance body by tapping meridian points.**

20. *Clean your hands with rubbing alcohol and proceed to close the crown. This releases trapped air so that the spirit and physical body fit together.*

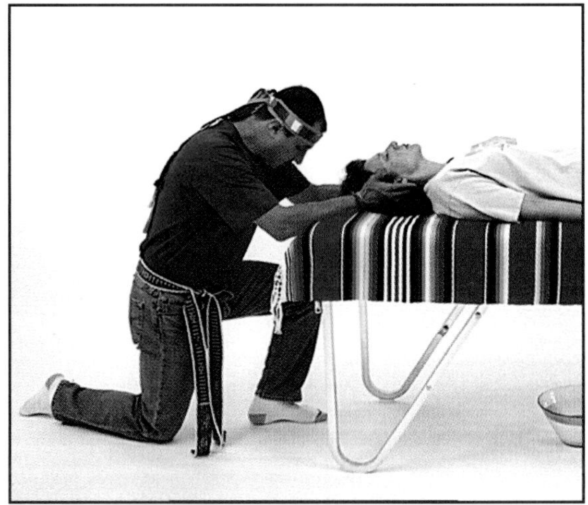

21. *Squeeze from back of head and inch upwards.*

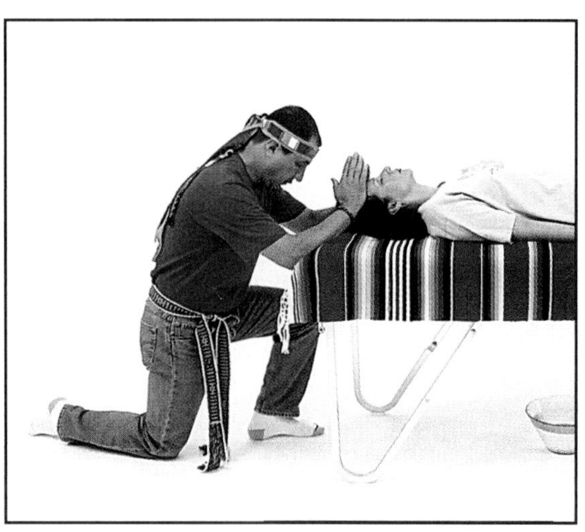

22. *Continue squeezing until you reach the front of head.*

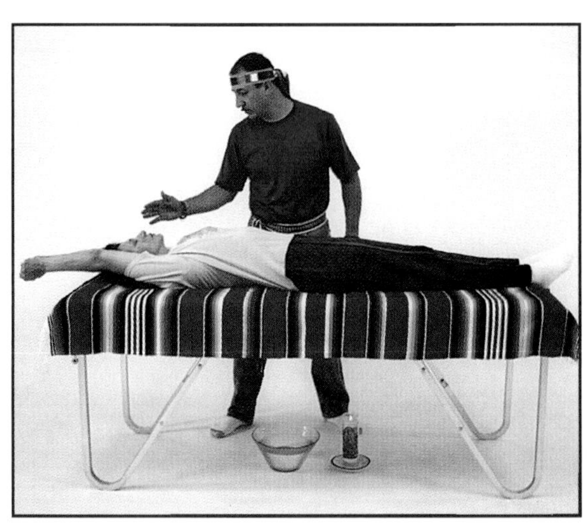

23. *Ask client to make a fist with his hands and stretch arms over his head.*

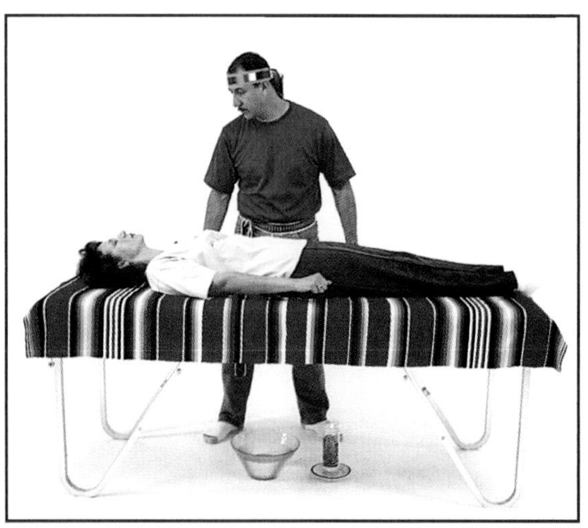

24. *Then have client bring his arms down to his sides.*

25. *Ask client to relax and breathe in and out deeply, once or twice.*

---

* Tapping meridian points is taught in my workshops.

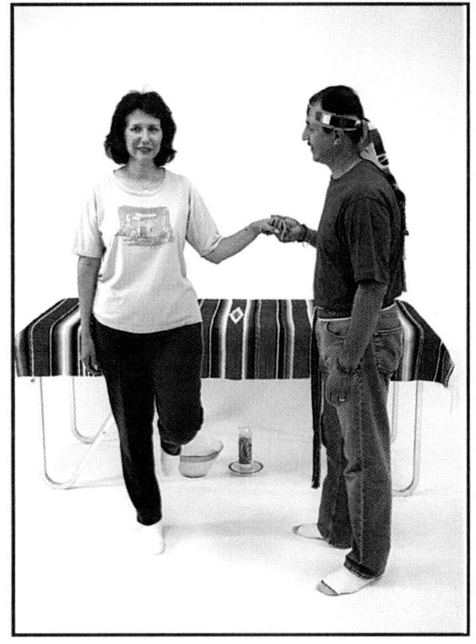

26. *Ask client to carefully stand, stomp the ground, flex fingers, and walk a bit forward, turn, and walk back.*

27. *Ask client how he feels.*

28. *Ask God to bless your client.*

29. *Cut your spiritual connection from your client.**

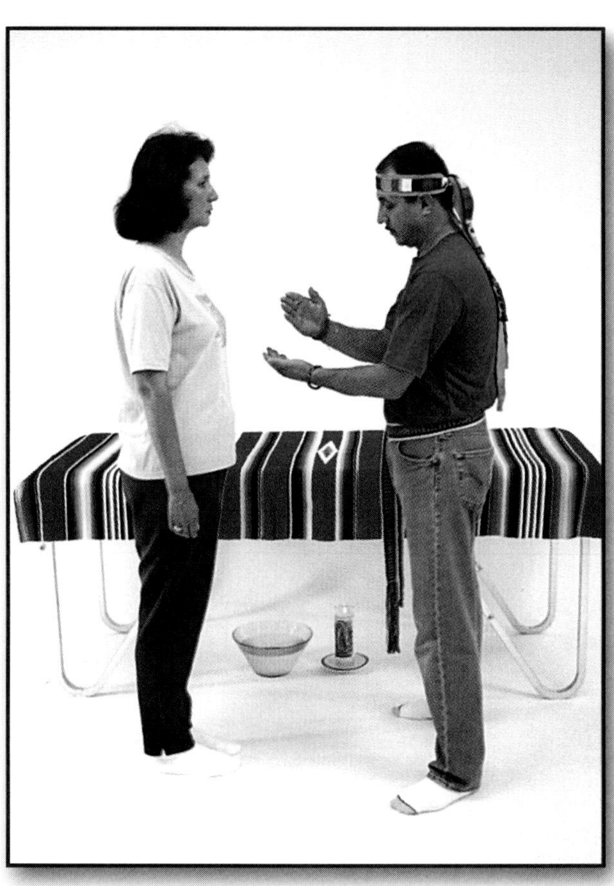

CAUTION: When your client is positive and has acceptance of self, spirit insertion will work easily. However, if your client does not wish to live, you, as a healer, must try to change his negative consciousness into a state of acceptance. This will facilitate Spirit Insertion.

* Cutting off energetically is taught in my workshops.

Chapter 3.6

GROUP SPIRIT INSERTION

1. *Use masking tape to mark a three (3) foot equilateral triangle on the floor. Bless the triangle before using.*
2. *Stand the client in the middle of the blessed triangle.*
3. *Select a group leader that will watch and guide everyone during Spirit Insertion.*

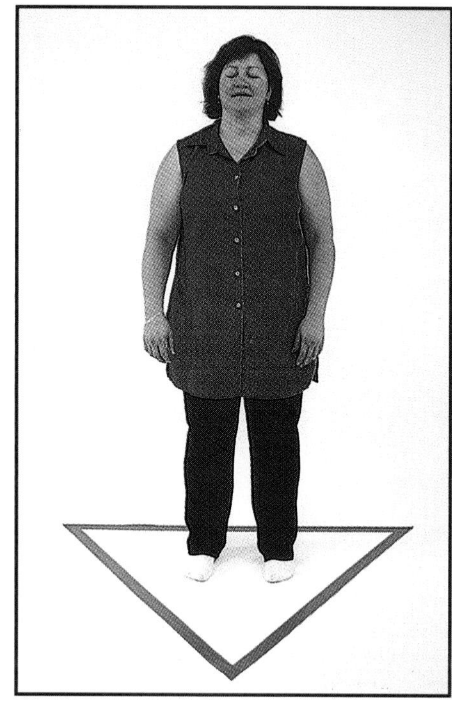

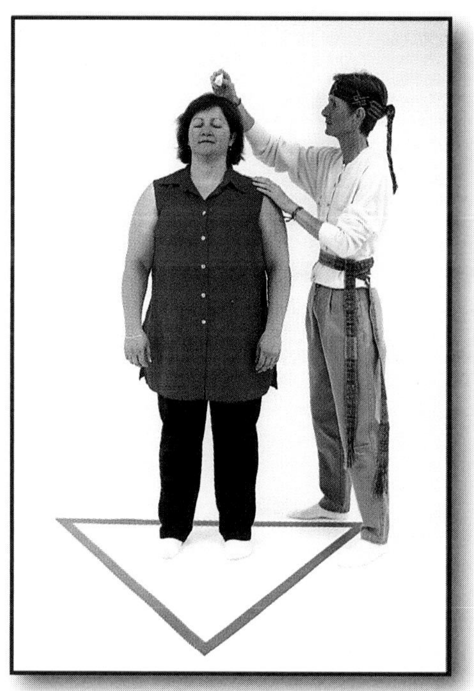

4. *A minimum of six (6) people should participate in Spirit Insertion.*
5. *Group leader applies blessed olive oil with a cotton ball to middle of client's head.*

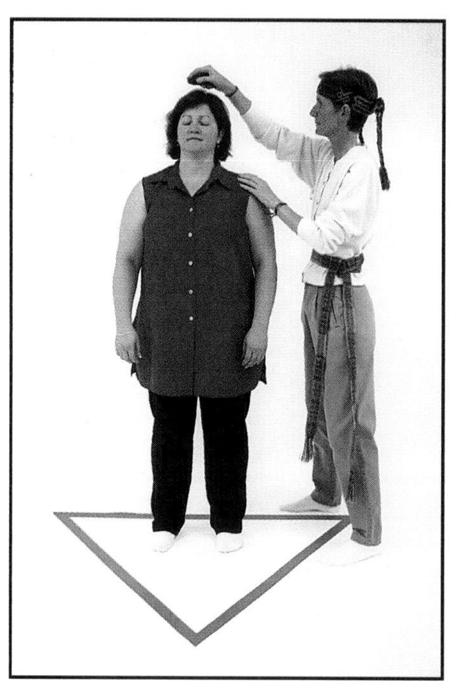

6. *The leader then makes three (3) spiritual incisions on client's head. The 1st incision is made in the name of God the Father; 2nd, in the name of God the Son; and the 3rd, in the name of God the Holy Spirit. (See cutting stone, p. 80, picture no. 3).*

7. *Group leader holds a blessed, lit, white candle above client's head to guide the client's spirit back into the physical body.*

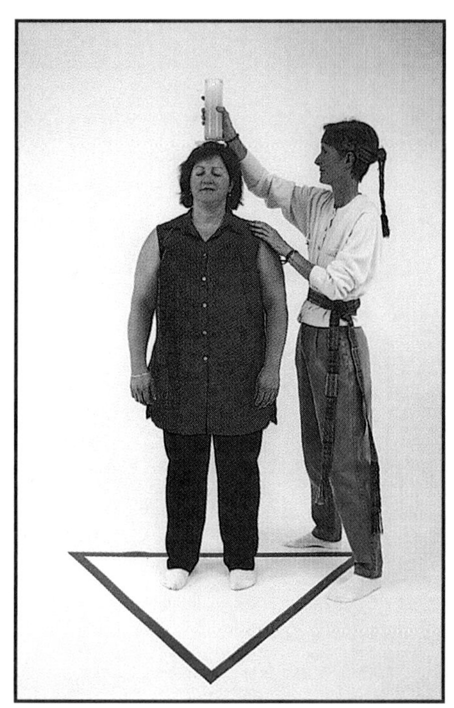

8. *Members of the healing group who feel called to do Spirit Insertion will stand with one foot touching blessed triangle while facing client.*

9. *Each healer raises one open hand above client's head and asks God's permission to insert the client's spirit.*

Do not participate in Spirit Insertion, if you do not feel the client's spirit in your hand.

Simply step back from the blessed triangle and give UNCONDITIONAL LOVE and COMPASSION to the client.
BE HUMBLE, NO EGO.
It's not your day.

Remind the client that his main focus is to keep GOD in his heart.

10. *When the spirit is received in healers' hands the group is ready for Spirit Insertion. They will close their hands and make a synchronized, clockwise motion above the client's head to gain momentum for insertion of spirit.*

11. *Ask your spirit guides to help. The leader and client then say out loud (from their hearts):*

Leader: "IN THE NAME OF GOD THE FATHER."

Client: "(FULL BIRTH NAME), I AM HERE."

Leader: "IN THE NAME OF GOD THE SON."

Client: "(FULL BIRTH NAME), I AM HERE."

Leader: "IN THE NAME OF GOD THE HOLY SPIRIT."

Client: "(FULL BIRTH NAME), I AM HERE."

12. *After the third call for spirit, the healers* ***simultaneously*** *pull the client's spirit downward into the client's body and then* ***simultaneously*** *slap the ground.*

13. *Bring client to "Present Time of Consciousness" (See Present Time of Consciousness procedure p. 105-106)*

14. *With clean hands, the group leader proceeds to close the client's crown chakra. Start from the back of the head then inch up the sides to the front of the head releasing trapped air. (See p. 107)*

15. *Keep burping out air* and allow the release to happen naturally. Don't try to do it yourself. Ask for spiritual guidance. Otherwise, find someone in your group that has the ability to release air naturally. This assures that the client's spirit is tight within his body.*

16. *Run your hands once firmly up and down the sides of your client's body to connect his flow of energy.*

17. *After Spirit Insertion, have client walk 10 to 15 steps. The group will feel, see or sense if Spirit Insertion was successful. The client will also respond with a reaction that cannot be denied. This process often brings tears of joy, happiness, and a sense of well-being.*

    If Spirit Insertion was not successful the first time, the group must attempt it a second time. Make sure that everyone works together ***as a team*** *for maximum spiritual strength.*

18. *Ask God for His final blessing for your client and everyone involved.*

CAUTION: **When your client is positive and has acceptance of self, spirit insertion will work easily. However, if your client does not wish to live, you, as a healer, must try to change their negative consciousness into a state of acceptance. This will facilitate spirit insertion.**

---

* There are healers who have the spiritual gift of releasing trapped air within the physical body. The trapped air, which causes physical pain, is released through loud burping. This form of extraction brings healing and adjustment to the physical body.

Chapter 3.7

DO WE ALWAYS NEED BOTH LEECH REMOVAL AND SPIRIT INSERTION HEALINGS?

We generally need both the leech removal and the spirit insertion healings. However, there is an exception. Although the percentage is very low, you may encounter someone who has leech attachment in the early stages. When this occurs the leech is caught in the outer portion of the energy field and the client's spirit has not yet shifted or moved out of his physical body.

While interviewing, always use the Symptoms Chart to help evaluate the condition of your client (Refer to p. 63). Use your intuition, spiritual guidance, and special gifts to confirm whether or not the client's spirit is out of his body. ***NEVER GUESS OR ASSUME ANYTHING.***

If you're not sure whether the client's spirit has shifted out of his body, but he does have leech attachment, perform both healings. Any spiritual healing given with good intent and God's blessing will not hurt a client in any way. When both healings are given, the client's symptoms will be corrected. But, if the symptoms continue, the problem may be:

1. Spirit insertion was done incorrectly (Refer to p. 102 and/or 109).

2. The condition is not spiritual. The problems may be on other levels such as:

a. physical b. mental c. emotional

In regards to No. 2, please refer your client to a medical physician, psychologist or psychiatrist to ensure appropriate treatment. Never forget that the highest level of integrity must always be present. Do not lose sight of the whole purpose of healing. These healings are intended to bring wellness and well-being to every human being that seeks help. Pray for those who can not seek help.

NOTES

UNCONDITIONAL LOVE

Chapter 3.8

AFTER A HEALING

I would like to share with you what most people experience after leech removal and spirit insertion healings. Most individuals regain their natural self and personality. It is a great feeling to see someone smile even though they may not truly understand what has taken place. This transformation is apparent to you and everyone else around them.

Changes occur on other levels as well, and most or all of the symptoms experienced prior to the healing are corrected (See **Symptoms Chart***, p. 45). Most importantly, the client regains his freedom of choice and will power. This is a miracle in itself.*

Equally important are the results associated with **spirit insertion***. Most of my clients notice an immediate improvement in their initial symptoms (See* **Spirit Out of Body Symptoms Chart***, p. 63). They also experience a heaviness in their feet. This heaviness is a feeling of touching and being grounded to Mother Earth. In addition, they experience a feeling of balance and well-being. These feelings are felt to the core of their being.*

I always give both healings in one session. It is **ALWAYS** *safer to perform both healings to ensure total recovery.*

You may rarely encounter a client who says he didn't feel anything happen during the healing. Even though you know the healing has taken place, give your client and yourself a 30-day waiting period to allow the healing to unfold. If, after 30 days, the client still feels no change, he has not yet recognized or accepted the healing. This may be due to lack of awareness or being in a state of denial. It is **never** *worth compromising your integrity. Refund their money.*

Chapter 3.9

RECOVERY PERIOD AFTER A HEALING

After every healing, I say to each client, "My wish for you is that you speak to God, that you love yourself, and that you forgive yourself. Bring no judgement of right or wrong to yourself or others. You must drink plenty of water and avoid all negative activities such as: television, radio, movies, computer games, loud music, etc".

The recovery period is a time of adjustment. It gives you the opportunity to return to your innocence. This helps you redefine who you really are. I ask that you not hide yourself, but surround yourself with the beauty that God has created for you. Be in harmony with yourself and everyone around you.

You are now safe to release all your blockages. Give yourself permission to experience everything that arises without questioning.

Remember to pray as it is very important. God desires that you, His children, communicate with Him. God listens to all prayers. If you don't pray, be sincere and speak from your heart. ***God the Father wants each of us to realize and know that we are never alone. God is all love and compassion.***

I have developed the following simple guidelines that I give to my clients after their healings. See 30-Day Recovery Period form that follows:

30-DAY RECOVERY PERIOD AFTER A HEALING

1. ***PRAY TO GOD IN YOUR OWN WAY.***

2. ***DURING THIS PERIOD OF HEALING, ALLOW YOUR FEELINGS TO FLOW WITHOUT QUESTIONING.***

3. ***FORGIVE YOURSELF.***

4. ***FORGIVE AND BLESS EVERYONE WHO HAS HURT YOU.***

5. ***LOVE YOURSELF AND OTHERS.***

6. ***HAVE A GOOD ATTITUDE.***

7. ***BE HAPPY.***

8. ***AVOID NEGATIVE TELEVISION, NEWS, LOUD MUSIC, AND OFFENSIVE LANGUAGE.***

9. ***AVOID RED MEATS, PORK, EGGS, BANANAS, CHILES, CAFFEINE, AND ALCOHOL.***

10. ***DRINK PLENTY OF WATER.***

11. ***TAKE MINERALS TO INCREASE THE EFFICIENCY OF YOUR BODY'S ELECTRICAL SYSTEM.***

If during the 30-day recovery period, you experience a recurrence of negative feelings, do not be alarmed. Give yourself an Epsom salt bath. * *This bath neutralizes your energy field. Soaking in the salt gets rid of trapped, dirty negative energy that is being released from your mental, physical, emotional, and spiritual bodies. When this dirty energy accumulates within your energy field, it will give you a false feeling of prior negative symptoms.*

If needed, repeat the Epsom salt bath once a week for 3 weeks. Continue to maintain a positive attitude and allow the 30-day healing period to run its course.

---

* See p. 128, No. 12

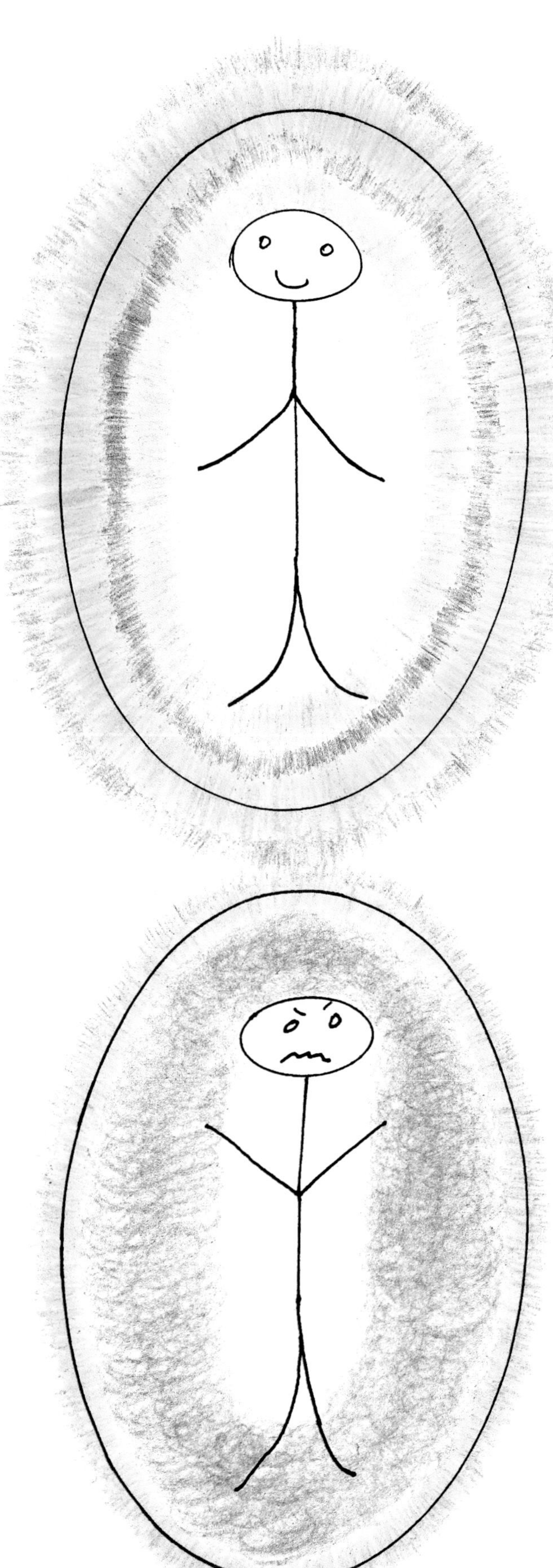

A clean energy field after a healing on all levels.

During and after the 30-day recovery period you should experience a natural high. This beautiful feeling can be maintained for a very long time.

During the recovery period false feelings and symptoms may be experienced.

Chapter 3.10

UNRESPONSIVE CLIENTS

During your healing career you may encounter a client who does not respond to any of your treatments. These clients are masters at hiding their emotions. These individuals may be:

1. *Shy*
2. *Introverted*
3. *Soft-spoken*
4. *Quiet*
5. *Traumatized*
6. *Intimidated*
7. *Fearful*
8. *In Denial*

As a healer, you have learned to expect a reaction or an acknowledgement from your client. When there is no reaction, you may start to experience:

1. *Doubt*
2. *Failure*
3. *Guilt*
4. *Bewilderment*

If these emotions start to surface, the healer must remain ***STRONG, CONFIDENT, and STEADFAST****. Do not let your client's unresponsiveness throw you off balance.* ***Trust*** *your intuition and inner guidance.* ***Have faith*** *that everything you asked for and gave was given spiritually.*

NOTES

UNCONDITIONAL LOVE

TO LOVE YOURSELF IS TO LOVE GOD
TO LOVE GOD IS TO LOVE YOURSELF

CHAPTER FOUR

Chapter 4

THE IMPORTANCE OF SPIRITUAL HEALER HYGIENE

In the early 70's, I devoted every spare moment to spiritual healings. During this period of time I encountered people filled with anger, revenge, hatred, and jealousy. Most of my spiritual healings consisted of witchcraft and leech removal. This was an exciting time for me because I learned and experienced first hand that leech attachments were out of control. Leech attachments became second to witchcraft removals.

I never questioned my guidance or my intuition. The help I received from my spirit guides was most valuable. I came to realize that a lit, white candle placed underneath my healing table was there to absorb all the negativity that was being released from my client. My beloved firestick is another blessed instrument that I have used for many years. With one sweep around the client's energy field I am able to cleanse and remove blocked negative energy.

Another hygiene technique that I used was to rub rock salt on the client's body to remove negative or dirty energy. This also protected me from absorbing any of the client's dirty energy into my own body. My spirit guides also instructed me to take a mixture of fresh lemon juice and pure olive oil before my daily healings as a protective agent for my physical body. After the last healing session of the day, one of my spirit guides always cleansed my physical body and cut all energetic connections to everyone that I had treated.

All of these above-mentioned practices may seem like small details, but they have helped me maintain a healthy, physical body. I have remained free from spiritual contamination, which has prevented me from experiencing healer burnout.

I have personally met many beautiful human beings who have a great desire to give healing to all humanity. Their heart is as big as the world; but after a few years of doing spiritual healings without using correct healer hygiene, these unique individuals experience chronic fatigue and death of their spirituality. This is what I call "healer burnout". They no longer want to know anything about spirituality. They have become disillusioned, withdrawn, and have lost faith in God and themselves.

A good spiritual healer must always maintain safe healer hygiene practices. *If not, the recovery period from healer burnout may take as long as ten years.*

Chapter 4.1

SPIRITUAL HYGIENE PRACTICES

1. *Abstain from alcohol and tobacco at least 24 hours before and 24 hours after a healing.*

2. *Designate certain clothes that will be used for all your healing sessions. This will prevent contaminating any of your other clothing.*

3. *A healer must drink a minimum of 12 ounces of water per client. This practice ensures your safety by continuously circulating your energy, thus preventing healer burnout.*

4. *Combine 1/2 freshly squeezed lemon and a tablespoon of virgin olive oil. Pray and ask for the drink to be blessed. Drink this mixture prior to starting your healing work for the day. The lemon mixture is used to protect the physical body from spiritual contamination. This drink is given to clients before a healing to assist in the removal of leeches.*

5. *Always have a white unscented candle burning while working.*

6. *Put 3-4 ounces of Epsom salt into a glass jar and fill with water. Place next to the candle or under your healing table.*

7. *Place sprigs of fresh rue under your blessed headbands and belts. This is to protect you from picking up unwanted energy.*

8. *Smoke your hands with incense before, during, and after a healing. This is to flush negative or dirty energy that is picked up through your hand chakras.*

9. *Cut off energetically after each client.*

10. *Wash your hands thoroughly after each healing with Epsom salt or plain salt and a lemon wedge. This will neutralize negative energy.*

11. *After a healing, do not talk about your client for 48 hours as you will reconnect with them energetically and interfere with their healing.*

12. *At least once a month, at night, place 2 cups of Epsom salt into your warm bath water and soak for 20 minutes.* This bath cleanses and neutralizes your energy field.*

---

* Avoid soaking more than 20 minutes as it will drain you.

13. *To re-energize yourself, cut 10 lemons into small pieces. Boil in large pot or container until soft. Let cool, then pour into blender and liquefy. Place into tub with warm water and soak for 20 minutes. Then shower as usual.*

14. ***"Switch On/Switch Off"*** *— When you are working you switch yourself* ***on*** *spiritually. When you are not working you switch yourself* ***off****. A fanatical healer is switched on 24 hours a day and always feels spacey. He is constantly seeing and experiencing spiritual information. He has a hard time functioning in reality. He is unable to separate his personal life from his spiritual life.*

How to Switch On

1. ***Pray to God.***
2. ***Connect to God's consciousness.***
3. ***State your intention to start all spiritual work.***

How to Switch Off

1. ***Say a closing prayer.***
2. ***State your intention to stop all spiritual work.***
3. ***Close your crown chakra and cut off energetically.***

Note: This material is part of a workshop I teach.

Chapter 4.2

HEALING ROOM HYGIENE

The healing room needs to be cleansed prior to and at the end of each working day. This is to prevent dirty energy from collecting in your workplace. A clean work area also helps the healer become aware of any spiritual intruder that can cause havoc during your healing. I recommend the following:

1. *Incense (frankincense) the healing area, your instruments, and table.*
2. *Light an unscented white candle.*
3. *Place a glass jar with Epsom salt and water next to the white candle or under your healing table.*
4. *Pray and ask God for blessings and protection for your healing area, yourself, and your instruments.*
5. *Always try to use the same healing place.*
6. *Treat your healing place with reverence and respect.*

Chapter 4.3

BRIDGING

Bridging is a process whereby the healer forms a connection to the client during a leech removal session. This spiritual connection is a bridge by which a leech can travel from the client and attach itself onto the healer's energy field. It is through the act of unconditional love and compassion that leech removal occurs. We must always practice caution when we are removing earthbound spirits.

It is during the release or "meltdown stage" where you, as a healer, are most vulnerable to bridging. I would now like to give you some examples of bridging.

1. ***Anger***

   Rose got very annoyed because Betty was out of sync with the rest of the healers. Rose's anger put herself and everyone else at risk even though her anger only lasted an instant. She immediately formed a bridge. The leech was attracted to her anger, which allowed it to cross the bridge and attach itself to Rose's energy field instead of going through the vortex of the Holy Cross.

2. ***Challenging***

   John attempted to do a leech removal by himself. Due to his ego he was unable to assess whether he had the spiritual strength to do the removal. He began challenging the leech in a condescending manner. His attitude easily formed a bridge. The leech recognized John's negative attitude, lack of self-love, and his big ego — all bait for the leech.

3. ***Clairsentient*** *(Sensitive to other's feelings)*

   Maria was working with her group one day and took the position at the top of the triangle, the position of God the Father. While standing in the triangle she began to feel all the client's emotions. Without realizing, Maria had stopped giving unconditional love and compassion, which connected her emotionally, thus creating a bridge.

4. ***Sympathetic*** *(Poor timing)*

   Amy got overly excited and embraced the client during the meltdown period. The bridge was formed and Amy gave herself a present.

5. ***Stepping Out of the Triangle***

   If for some reason you need to leave the triangle, stop giving unconditional love and light for a cool-down period of 1-3 minutes before stepping out. If you step out of the triangle before the cool-down period is completed, you will form a bridge.

6. ***Negativity***

   Rita came in to participate in a healing session with a negative attitude, which empowered the leeches. Negative thoughts, attitudes, and emotions all act like big magnets to form bridges and attract leeches to your energy field.

To attempt leech removal you must be armed with unconditional love, compassion, humility, honesty, and integrity. Again, I stress it is crucial that healers in healing groups understand the value of teamwork. They must also respect each other's gifts.

We all have valuable contributions to share. We must work honestly and acknowledge our own strengths and weaknesses so as not to put ourselves and others in jeopardy. Just because you are a male healer and have male strength does not mean you are a better healer than your female counterpart.

Remember, leeches know everything about you. You cannot lie or pretend. Just because they are not seen by most, does not mean they cannot see and know everything about you. They know if you are fearful or pretending to be some great healer when you are not. Everyone must be treated with love and respect whether they are in spirit or physical form. ***We are all God's children.***

CAUTION: Always cut your spiritual connection after every healing.

NOTES

UNCONDITIONAL LOVE

ASK GOD TO FORGIVE YOU

CHAPTER FIVE

Chapter 5

SPIRITUAL HEALERS

An outstanding spiritual healer is committed to God, has faith, and unconditional love for humanity. Anyone without these three attributes will have limited results. Your accumulated knowledge and experience is good. However, without God's intervention, you are limiting your healing potential.

A spiritual healer has been blessed by the Holy Spirit and given the gift of healing. There are many individuals who share similar abilities or duties. Not one individual has all the gifts. There are, of course, many different types and levels of gifts and faculties.

If I were to seek a spiritual healer, I would want someone balanced in all areas of his life. I would look for someone who is:

Sincere	*Responsible*	*Generous*
Honest	*Approachable*	*Confident*
Easy Going	*A Good Listener*	*Dedicated*

My healer must also have the following:

Faith	*Integrity*	*Compassion*
Humility	*Steadfastness*	*Patience*
Wisdom	*Understanding*	*Knowledge*
	A Good Sense of Humor	

As a healer, I have a very strong relationship with God, which gives me my foundation of spiritual strength. I have faith, integrity, and unconditional love for humanity.

I would like to share these thoughts from the deepest part of me, my soul:

The flower cannot exist without soil or water.
I, the instrument, cannot work much less exist without God and faith.

La flor no puede existir sin tierra ni agua.
Yo, el instrumento, sin Dios y fe no puedo trabajar ni existir.

Chapter 5.1

DIFFERENT TYPES OF HEALERS AND THEIR GIFTS

Natural Born Healers

Most natural born healers in every culture perform a little bit of everything. The most common spiritual healing is witchcraft removal. Some natural born healers have been traditionally trained while others have never received any formal training or read a book about the healing gift they practice. These individuals simply respond to the problem or situation that presents itself.

During my many years of healing I have had the pleasure of meeting some natural born healers with various spiritual gifts. But, they have chosen not to use them. It has been my experience that when these healers do not use their gifts, their lives become very challenging and full of tribulations.

Many natural born healers cannot tell the difference between a leech and witchcraft. They treat both conditions in the same manner when in fact they are two different healings. Unaware that leeches can be removed with the act of unconditional love rather than force, these healers forcefully remove leeches and leave them in limbo or darkness. This is due to their lack of training or knowledge.

Situations such as witchcraft may or will require a little more force depending upon the healer's spiritual strength. ***It is always imperative that you, as a healer, interpret your perception or guidance carefully in each situation.***

Recall / Faith Healing

Not all healers have spirit guides. Some individuals are gifted with what I call, "recall." These individuals recall from many past life times their individual strength of love, compassion, and commitment with God, which gives them the spiritual strength in the present time of consciousness. Sometimes this recall happens automatically and other times the healer must ask for it every time they perform a spiritual healing. This gift can be awakened in early childhood or later in life.

This recall can also be interpreted as faith healing. What makes the healing possible is that the healer is in love with God and self and is then able to share that love of God with humanity.

Faith healers amplify God's love and compassion, which then allows the Holy Spirit to illuminate their physical being to provide the miracle. Some faith healers have spirit guides while others have Angelic assistance. Other faith healers have both Angelic and spirit guide assistance depending upon the extent of their gift and purpose in this present lifetime.

When a person is praying, meditating, and asking for a spirit guide, he must be aware of the **huge** *responsibility that comes with his request. A spirit guide will amplify all of the healer's worst fears, attitudes, and insecurities. These issues will come up all at once. The amplification allows the healer to come face to face with all his negative human tendencies. During this time frame or "window period" (5 years) he is given the opportunity to overcome his issues and become a cleaner instrument so that he can eventually work with spirit guides of high frequency.*

There are only two choices during this window period. The first choice for the healer is to go into denial about his issues, retreat inward, and continue wallowing in all his insecurities. Or, he can choose to **face** *and* **deal** *with his issues through love, trust, and acceptance of who he is in this present time of consciousness. He can then make the necessary changes and ultimately live life to the fullest and fulfill his purpose of serving humanity.*

Spirit Guides

Spirit guides are given to a healer by God. Both healer and spirit guide have specific tasks to perform to help humanity. The gift that the healer appears to have is actually the seal or gift that has come with his spirit guide. For example, if the gift of the spirit guide is to remove negativity, that is the gift of the healer. All information and knowledge regarding this gift becomes the healer's specialty provided it is being used regularly. Sometimes the healer may have the ability to do other healings as well. However, these modalities are still not his specialty. The healer will generally attract those individuals with problems associated with his specialty.

Full Mediums

A full medium is an individual who has been blessed with the gift of separating his spirit from his physical body. When this occurs, the medium enters a state of ecstasy and elevates his spirit to God for safekeeping. At this time, his body then becomes an instrument utilized by a spirit guide of high frequency in God's consciousness. The guide is sent to help humanity, provide knowledge, awareness, and healing as allowed by God.

Different levels exist in mediumship. This gift is granted according to the healer's level of spiritual evolution. At this time, there are few individuals with genuine, full mediumships. However, there are a large percentage of individuals that are coming into age with this gift. These individuals must remain healthy in mind, body, and spirit and let go of all or most of their negative human tendencies. These choices allow their true natural selves to flow and amplify more of their honorable traits such as humility, unconditional love, and being non-judgmental. They must also maintain a constant relationship and understanding of God.

Those individuals with the gift of full mediumship have what I call the "keeper of the crown" (the spirit guide who protects the instrument from any negative or addictive intruders).

The keeper of the crown also has the duty of cleaning the instrument before leaving. This ensures good healer hygiene.

STANDARD SPIRITUAL PROCEDURE: (KEEPER OF THE CROWN)

1. *Enters host body*
2. *Protects host body from intruders*
3. *Greets everyone and opens the session*
4. *Works with instrument to provide guidance/healing*
5. *Blesses everyone*
6. *Cleanses instrument*
7. *Departs only when instrument's spirit is ready to move in*

Please note that it is not how many books you read about mediumship or how much you practice channeling in a group that qualifies you for this gift. What separates a true medium from those that read, attend lectures and/or pretend to have this gift, is the seal and mark that is given to the medium or healer by God. All those having the gift of vision will see the guide very clearly. For those who do not have the gift of vision, they will know the medium is real because they will receive a feeling that touches the core of their soul. They will know without a doubt that they have felt the truth about that medium.

Not all mediums have the gift of releasing earthbound spirits from a host body. It depends on the individual gift of the spirit guide of high frequency and the medium.

However, both play a role in assisting groups of healers who are removing addictive earthbound spirits. Unconditional love is amplified through the medium, thus making it possible for these beautiful healings to take place at an accelerated pace and with more accuracy.

<u>Half Medium</u>

A half medium has the ability to remain partially within his body while allowing spirit to channel. He is aware of what is being said and done in both realities simultaneously. This special gift can sometimes be more than an individual can carry. A half medium must do the following in order to be successful:

1. *Surrender his mind and heart to God for safekeeping*
2. *Follow Spiritual Laws of God*
3. *Allow Spirit Guide of high frequency to serve humanity*
4. *Remember he is only an instrument*

Not following these steps will result in the instrument falling from grace. It is a natural human tendency to want to participate in what is being said by Spirit. When ego is allowed to manifest, it will interfere with spirit guide communication, thus causing distortions and possible crown chakra blockage. For example: during the time a medium is channeling, spirit guide of high frequency is amplifying all of the instrument's insecurities. A risk factor may develop that can cause the medium to block spirit guide communication. The danger is that the medium may substitute his own words (consciousness).

The gift of a half medium is very challenging. The challenges are so over-whelming that these potential healers may become introverted, and may abandon their true calling. Many potential half mediums have not dealt with their insecurities and bad attitudes. They project their own individual personality and mental consciousness. They have not yet accepted or truly known God.

They must understand that they are an instrument of God and are in service to humanity. This gift is to be treated with total respect and dignity. Mediumship is not a game or something to be taken lightly. To do so would be to create "bad karma."

Do not be quick to desire any level of mediumship. This gift comes with great responsibility. At times you may feel the weight of the world on your shoulders. You must always maintain constant communication with God, have unbreakable faith and integrity, and display all of your honorable attributes during your spiritual service. All these traits must be carried over into every aspect of your personal life.

There are many different categories and variations of half mediums. Each will have a unique way of helping humanity. Not all full mediums, half mediums, and spiritual healers have the same gifts. There are many different levels and gifts. Again, **do not assume** *that every spiritual healer has the ability to remove witchcraft or addictive earthbound spirits.* ***You*** *must find that particular individual that has this gift and blessing.*

Human Beings Impersonating A Spirit Guide

There are individuals who believe they can channel. They impersonate a spirit guide unaware that this gift of mediumship is given by God. In a distorted way, these individuals are so hungry for spirituality that they will do anything to be included or accepted as being spiritual.

Those who impersonate spirit guides are being dishonest and lack integrity. Worst of all, they have committed a sacrilege by disrespecting the spiritual laws of God. Thus, innocent people who seek guidance become vulnerable and often fall victim to these imposters.

Spirit impersonation has always existed. It has been my personal observation that mental confusion arises due to an abundance of information received during a window period while on the path of spirituality.

There are two types of spirit impersonations:

1. *Spirits Impersonating Humans*
2. *Spirits Impersonating Other Spirits*

Spirits Impersonating Humans

Example: Many claim to have the gifts of hearing and seeing when in truth they are only perceiving the spirit world. Negative spirits know this and take advantage. They turn this against you by using false information concerning someone you care about.

Spirits Impersonating Other Spirits

Negative spirits and leeches can also impersonate departed souls and spirits of light. When a negative spirit or leech impersonates, it creates a disturbance. This disturbance leads to confusion, which causes a distancing from those who can help you.

These negative spirits and leeches will appeal to your sympathies by working their miracles of delusion....that's when they know they have you.

Spirit Impersonation Versus the Truth

It is important to remember that you have one advantage over negative spirits and leeches — ***YOU KNOW THE TRUTH****. You know the integrity and personality of the person being spoken about.*

Take time to evaluate the information you have perceived. When the information is wrong, you will have distortions, fragmented thought forms, and gaps. These are good indications that you have attracted a negative spirit.

*These warning signs should **NEVER** be ignored. Staying in integrity and interpreting the information correctly is your responsibility. **NEVER LOSE SIGHT OF THE TRUTH!***

Spirit Communication with the Departed

I feel that it is important to mention that there are gifted individuals who can perceive and sometimes even see spirits of the deceased. These gifted individuals have helped many grief-stricken families and friends by providing profound, heart-felt, and accurate information that brings healing and closure to all parties involved.

Energy Healing

Energy healing is based upon the intent of the sender. The healer utilizes his consciousness / mind as a vehicle to deliver the healing. This type of healing is very strong. Again, it depends on the moral integrity of the healer. It is a different avenue of healing. Not everyone's capability is the same. The effectiveness of the healing can vary tremendously.

Do not attempt to utilize transference of energy techniques in trying to remove addictive earthbound spirits. This technique will not succeed. If you try, you may hurt the host body by overcharging the energy field or parts of it. The client will temporarily feel energized, but after a period of time the original symptoms will manifest again or worsen. The overcharging allows the leeches to feed upon the excess energy that the healer has transferred into the client's aura. In addition, if a healer is negative he will amplify the negative traits already possessed by the leeches. This will in turn create more havoc for the client.

Transference of energy, when used correctly, can bring about wellness and well-being. The effectiveness of the transference of energy depends upon the healer's attitude, consciousness, and whether he prays for God's guidance.

Chapter 5.2

HOW TO IDENTIFY A GOOD HEALER

As a client, it is very important to research various types of healers in the market place so that your specific condition(s) or symptoms may be healed. Your search may be overwhelming because healer's expertise and levels vary.

When you locate the healer that can best accommodate your needs, never assume that he has all the answers or that he can identify or pinpoint all your problems. One of the safest ways for locating a good healer is to look for an individual with the highest degree of integrity, faith, and love for God.

How do you know when you have met this individual? There is a feeling within your entire being that recognizes his humility. The healer's act of unconditional love is so evident that it radiates and surrounds him. His unconditional love is an undeniable feeling that reaches the core of your being. His attitude and persona will be most inviting.

A healer who has integrity and is an instrument of God will never put you in a compromising position whereby he can gain from your vulnerability. If any healer suggests or requires you to submit to sexual acts in order to receive a healing, ***this is not of God's will****. Even though you are in a desperate situation, never allow yourself to be abused or robbed of your dignity. These negative or distorted healers are common in our society.*

Healers who are with God and stand in righteousness have no obstacles that prohibit them from providing the necessary healing. These individuals are blessed to work beyond our three-dimensional reality. It is a reality in which they are able to utilize different doors to accommodate the individual. One thing is for sure, this individual will always tell you the truth. If he is unable to give you the necessary treatment, he will be humble enough to recommend another healer or guide you in the right direction.

BE SIMPLE

CHAPTER SIX

Chapter 6

TESTIMONIALS

I have chosen a few testimonials from the many I have collected over the years. The testimonials were selected to give you a clear understanding of the many profound changes that my clients have experienced on different levels. Given the fact that their experiences are highly personal and sensitive in nature, I felt it necessary to conceal their identities to protect their privacy.

As my client's testimonials were rather lengthy and repetitive, I have edited them to provide clarity.

One-hour Private Session (Faith Healing)

Name: M. J.

Nine and a half years ago I had an 8-hour neck resection operation to remove malignant cancer from both sides of my neck. This operation was followed by three weeks of radiation therapy. The radiation badly damaged the enamel on all my teeth and restricted the blood flow within both jawbones. It also destroyed my taste buds and salivary glands. I was diagnosed with xerostomia or dry mouth.

During this period I was forced to spray artificial saliva into my mouth throughout the day and several times during the night. I met Victor Barron for the first time while having a personal one-hour session with him. Six days later, I found my mouth becoming moist without the use of the artificial saliva spray. Within two weeks, my salivary glands gradually produced more moisture and are now working at approximately 80% capacity. I have not used the saliva spray since Victor's healing. Without reservation, I would recommend any person with a physical or emotional problem to contact Victor for help.

Symptoms: The client came in with an illness called xerostomia or dry mouth. He wore a neck brace to support his head because doctors feared that his brittle trachea would break. His skin was discolored from the lower jaw down through his shoulders and upper chest area. The skin was stretched and leathery looking; and when I touched it, it felt hard.

Treatment: I had M.J. lie down on the healing table and anointed him with blessed oil. At that moment, I knelt and petitioned to God my Father asking Him for a miracle. I prayed that M.J.'s salivary glands again produce saliva.

I then sang to God in Spanish. I had an overwhelming feeling of unconditional love for M.J. I stood up and touched the affected areas as I continued singing.

One-hour Private Session

Name: I. M.

I asked for a healing on an old bruise that had been on my shin for 30 years. The bruise had given me constant pain over the past six years.

After Victor's healing I had a feeling of well-being and peace of mind. I now have a dull feeling in my shin, but the pain is gone.

One-hour Private Session

Name: J. J.

Symptoms: Severe neck pain, lower back problems, back stiffness when walking or sitting, shaky hand, trouble sleeping, bad dreams, depression, anxiety, and trouble in relationships.

Treatment and Results: I was able to determine that she was possessed and a leech had a very tight grip on her. It was not the normal attachment I usually encounter. I looked into her cellular level and there I found the intruder. I asked the client to visualize all of her cells shaking at a high speed. At that moment, I asked Christ to manifest Himself in every cell in her body.

Shortly after, the manifestation of a dark shadow began to appear. She said she could feel something behind her. I quickly went behind her and pulled the leech off of her. She also experienced a sharp pain in the nape area, which was very uncomfortable. I went in spiritually with my hand and pulled out what was left of the leech. Instantly she felt very good.

Once again, I spiritually cleansed her entire body. Then I asked the Lord's permission to insert her spirit. When spirit insertion had taken place, she said, "I feel myself again. I had forgotten how this felt. I feel so good!" Within a few minutes she was so happy she could not stop smiling. She also was emotional and said, "I feel free."

15-minute Session

Name: L. M.

It's been exactly one year since I lost my soulmate. My heart was heavy and I was very sad and distressed. I was carrying a lot of emotional pain. I could feel a lot of negative energy. I was broken physically, emotionally, and spiritually.

After my healing with Victor, I felt an immediate inner release. My energies were lifted. I felt I had a "new lease on life." I had an emotional high and now felt I could go on. After I left the Expo, I went to Mass and for the first time in a year I was able to attend without sorrow and crying. I felt God's light enter my soul.

One-hour Private Session to remove witchcraft

Name: W. C.

Symptoms: Head pain, irritable, nervous, pain in the spine and legs, unable to concentrate, couldn't sleep, low energy, very negative, bad attitude at work, and pain throughout the body.

Evaluation: There were leech attachments along the spine and on his energy field. His spirit was out and he was not in his present time of consciousness. He also had witchcraft for approximately 25 years.

Treatment: With blessed oil I anointed W. C. with the sign of the cross. I used the Holy Cross to open the gateway and had him stand in front of it. I gave him unconditional love to start the healing process and he reacted immediately with great pain in his body.

Each time I extracted a leech from W. C. he would momentarily lose control of his body and his emotions. He felt severe rage and wanted to strike me.

After removing all the leeches, I removed the witchcraft and inserted his spirit into his body. I then brought him back to the present time of consciousness, which allowed him to regain his natural state. I ended the session with a blessing.

15-minute Session

Name: S. A.

After a decade of being clean and sober, I felt like something was blocking me from moving forward in my new way of life. I wanted to share my experiences with others to help them reach their "higher good."

Victor pulled some sort of negative energy out of my body and cleansed every cell. He used his body like a vacuum and I was free. God talked to me that day through Victor and told me to go forward and be myself. He placed the keys of life in my palm and I put them into my heart.

I feel nothing can stop me now. I was reminded by God how brave I have been through my trials and what a powerful goddess I am. Thank you, Victor.

Healing on a child during one of my workshops

Name: L. K.

Symptoms: For several years the client had been growing more depressed and withdrawn. He had a lot of anger and frustration, which seemed out of proportion to his life's experiences. Recently, he felt life wasn't worth living and spoke several times of killing himself. There was a lot of tension and a feeling of a black cloud hovering over his home.

Treatment: During a team effort, I stepped in to assist. I removed the leeches and finished cleansing his energy field.

Results: The mother testified that immediately after the healing, her son's face looked more relaxed. His eyes were open and sparkling instead of veiled and dull. His behavior since the healing has been much more affectionate and lively. The barriers of darkness around him are gone.

One-hour Private Session

Name: E. R.

I have been in spiritual warfare for many years. I sought help from the Catholic Church. The priests were sympathetic, but after numerous deliverance sessions they were unable to help. Throughout this time, I was conscious of the influence of the dark side. I acquired a strong faith, which sustained me over the last 15 years. After reading an article in the local paper about Victor and his extraordinary gifts, I felt confident that he would be able to help.

As Victor began his healing, I was aware of his strong faith in God. He feared no evil as he encountered great resistance. For the first time since dealing with the dark side, I knew that Victor had the knowledge, strength, and experience to set me free. He was in total control. I knew that he had indeed been chosen by God to do this extraordinary work. Thank you, Victor. God bless you.

Healing during a Shaman Workshop

Name: J. M.

Student of Anthropology. She attended this workshop as part of a class project.

I most enjoyed being able to participate in the hands-on experience during this workshop. I found Victor's humility and sincerity deeply inspiring.

This class was a fascinating introduction for me to see the healing work of a Shaman. I respect Victor and his work. Victor has helped me understand that I have much to learn. I am very grateful for the opportunity to attend this workshop.

One-hour Private Session

Name: P. G.

For five months I saw numerous doctors yet none were able to pinpoint my medical condition. They all wanted to operate. They would say that maybe it was my gallbladder, liver, etc.

I hated the sight of myself. I would cut out my head from photos because of the terrible, piercing stare I saw in my eyes. I couldn't even stand looking at myself in the mirror when shaving.

About two months ago I saw two dogs. I stared at them with so much anger they came to attack me. I just kept staring at them. As one of them came to bite me, I picked up two good-sized rocks. I hit the dog two times with a lot of rage. My anger was uncontrollable. When I finally realized what I was doing, I remembered I had my eight-year-old niece with me. She was very scared and could have been hurt.

My symptoms were: antisocial behavior, change in personality, high and low energies, and bad dreams. People would visit and everything would bother me. My wife would say I needed to control my bad attitude so I would just go outside. It got to the point that I did not want to be in my own home with my family. I told my wife several times I just wanted to die so that I could have some peace.

Treatment: Victor asked me to look into his eyes. He then blessed me and I felt something begin to move in my body. He asked me to close my eyes. I experienced pain in my stomach area. As Victor touched me and began pushing upward on my stomach, I felt something ugly coming up. As Victor pulled it out of my mouth it left a sulfur-like taste. My eyes sprung open immediately and I could see clearly. My rage was gone. I wanted to run and jump. The joy I felt was unexplainable.

RECOMMENDED READING

Carter, Mary Ellen, Under the Editorship of Hugh Lynn Cayce, *Edgar Cayce Modern Prophet*, A.R.E. Press, Virginia Beach, VA 1967.

Carter, Mary Ellen and McGarey, William A., *Edgar Cayce on Healing*, Aquarian Press, New York, NY 1972.

Carter, Mary Ellen and McGarey, William A., *Edgar Cayce on Healing*, Aquarian Press, New York, NY 1991.

Cayce, Edgar Evans, *Edgar Cayce on Atlantis*, Time Warner Books, New York, NY 1968.

Fiore, Edith, Ph.D., *The Unquiet Dead*, Ballantine Books, New York, NY 1987.

Kirkwood, Annie, *Mary's Message of Hope*, Blue Dolphin Publishing, Inc., Nevada City, CA 1995.

Kok Sui, Choa, *Pranic Healing*, Samuel Weiser, Inc., York Beach, ME 1990.

Pellegrino-Estrich, Robert, *The Miracle Man*, Triad Publishers Pty. Ltd., Cairns, Qld., Australia 1997.

Scallion, Gordon-Michael, *Notes from the Cosmos*, Matrix Institute, Inc., Chesterfield, NH 1997.

Starr, Aloa, *Prisoners of Earth*, Light Technology Publishing, Sedona, AZ 1993.

APPENDIX

During my many years of leech removal I have been blessed to develop various other leech removal techniques. My methods are taught during group or individual training sessions. The skills I teach require hands-on training to ensure that all steps are followed correctly so that you do not hurt yourself or anyone else.

I offer a quarterly Calendar of Events that includes dates for my meditations, unfoldings, and all workshops that I will conduct at the Body, Mind and Spirit Healing Center, in Whittier, California (a suburb of Los Angeles). I also organize Spiritual Retreats for those who are interested (See mail-in tear off).

I am currently offering the following Workshops and Spiritual Retreat:

ATTUNEMENT WORKSHOP * *Prerequisite*

When the polarity of the planet shifts many are going to experience physical and mental traumas. During this period of earth's adjustments, it is imperative for everyone to be able to sustain balance and normality on their physical, mental, and spiritual levels. Learn how to balance yourself for earth's magnetic changes. By using this attunement exercise daily you can create a temporary soul energy field that can be reactivated at anytime to sustain you. Learn how to help yourself, family, and friends.

* *Prerequisite: The **Color Workshop** is designed to help you know and feel the essence of who you really are and get to know your vibrational frequency and color. This course will help prepare you to make the connection when you learn **The Attunement**.*

CANDLE PREPARATION FOR HEALING AND PROTECTION WORKSHOP

A simple, yet intensive, one-day candle workshop that will assist everyone during these challenging times. You will learn a special prayer that will invoke God's blessings before doing the candle preparation. Various colored candles will be used in combinations for such things as: protection against negativity, breaking spells, and healings for yourself and others.

CHAKRA HARMONIZING WORKSHOP

In a relaxed atmosphere that will give you plenty of hands-on practice you will learn how to work with all the major chakras. This workshop is recommended for all beginners. If you are already practicing the healing arts, this class will increase your effectiveness as a healer.

Easy to learn step-by-step techniques for:

- Opening/cleansing all chakras individually
- Repairing damaged chakras
- Replacing webs and filters inside chakras
- Learning how to extract negative thought forms
- Identifying malfunctioning and/or irregular chakras

COLOR VIBRATION WORKSHOP

In this workshop you will discover your soul's color frequency in which you are resonating in this present time of consciousness. As a bonus, you will learn the difference between your negative and positive traits so that you can achieve balance in your life.

EMBRACE YOURSELF AND MEET YOUR GUARDIAN ANGEL WORKSHOP

You will be assisted to the door, which will enable you to develop an ongoing relationship with your Guardian Angel. The benefits you will receive are as follows:

1) Enriches and deepens your spiritual life
2) Releases energy blocks that have kept you in self-denial
3) Diffuses negative emotions and limitations, thereby allowing your heart to open again
4) Two days of intensive releasing, clearing, and healing

Once the clearing has been done you are now ready to feel, sense or perceive information in thought forms and possibly even hear a celestial voice....gifts to humanity from God! It's your Guardian Angels' way of personally connecting with you.

HANDS-ON SPIRITUAL HEALING WORKSHOP

This workshop awakens your healing abilities if you are a beginner, and increases your effectiveness if you are already practicing the healing arts. All healers will work on the energy body and not the physical body.

Learn step by step techniques for:

1) Learning to feel the healing energy in your hands and physical body
2) Self-healing techniques
3) Distance healing
4) Asking for God's guidance
5) Learning how to relieve many minor discomforts
6) Healer hygiene to avoid healer burnout
7) Hands-on practice

KNOWING & WORKING WITH SPIRIT GUIDES WORKSHOP

It is *critical* to know who or what you are INVOKING — ***Are you helping or harming others?***
Remember — Universal energy consists of everything positive and negative.

An intensive one-day workshop of *feeling and connecting* with spirits of high frequency through the traditional unfolding process; a practice that has been unavailable to Western knowledge until now. This is an important workshop for all: beginners, advanced healers, clairvoyants, spiritual workers, etc.

Benefits:

- Gain spiritual strength and awareness
- Learn how to distinguish between high and low frequency spirits
- Discern how to receive guidance from high frequency spirits only
- Learn how to protect yourself

LEECH REMOVAL WORKSHOP

An intensive weekend workshop that will teach you about addictive earthbound spirits, or as I call them *Leeches*. Leeches are human beings who are in spirit form and desire to experience their negative human tendencies by attaching themselves to a host body in our physical plane.

You will learn how to identify and differentiate negative energies, witchcraft, and addictive earthbound spirits. You will then learn how to safely and effectively remove leeches by using the techniques/methods shown and taught to me by my Spirit Guides. This workshop requires **TEAMWORK**.

MAGNETIC GRID BALANCING AND CORRECTIONS WORKSHOP

I was given an insight into a spiritual method for doing what is commonly known as Feng Shui and have developed a one-day intensive workshop. This workshop is designed to help and assist with the corrections of earth's magnetic energy flow. You will be taught simple techniques and receive a special blessing from God. By working as a **team**, you will be able to save clients costly remodeling expenses on their homes or offices.

The following benefits are included:

- Removes bad and stagnated energy
- Repairs and corrects magnetic tears in the earth's grids
- Restores harmony, health, and peace within your environment, which allows for a constant flow of positive energy

TRADITIONAL SHAMAN HEALING WORKSHOP

A powerful one-day workshop designed to teach three indigenous spiritual healings (one for good luck, one for emotional pain, and a traditional healing). You'll perform the actual healings using various raw materials, plants, herbs, and fire in a friendly learning atmosphere. These healings are very powerful and have an immediate effect upon the physical body before slowly filtering out to work on the spiritual body. If you are already a practitioner in the healing arts, these healing techniques will enhance your existing work.

SPIRITUAL RETREAT

Join us and enjoy an all-inclusive Shamanic Retreat and experience (4) spiritual healings involving all the elements of nature. First, ***Mother Earth*** will embrace you and allow you to become one with her. This healing entails a profound cleansing and releasing of negative energies and unwanted issues. You will then ask permission from the ***Spirit of the River*** to allow you to enter its sacred water and receive a cleansing and purification of your entire being.

Next, you will go into the ***Circle of Life*** to release additional, unwanted issues and face the truth of who you are on all levels of consciousness, in all dimensions. Walking within the Circle of Life allows for changes and growth within yourself.

The last sacred ceremony, ***The Sweatlodge***, is a very profound and emotional experience, which allows you to come face to face with your Creator, "The Great Spirit", to receive His blessings, His strength, and His encouragement to undergo your final, spiritual trial. The Sweatlodge will release many blockages from your cellular memory. These releases will prepare you to receive your vision, inner knowing or direction for your own personal life. As the Sweatlodge nears its conclusion, you will experience total love and oneness with God/Creator.

Compassion

AVAILABLE SERVICES

1. Spiritual Healing, Private Session (1-hour)

2. Spiritual Healing, Phone Session (15-min.)

3. Spiritual Healing, Mini-Session (15-min.)

4. Cleansing and Blessing of Your Home (removal of negative spirits and witchcraft included). An additional $50.00 will be charged for each individual living in the home who wants a spiritual healing. Travel time extra.

5. Magnetic Grid Balancing, Cleansing, and Blessing of Your Home (removal of negative spirits and witchcraft included). Fee determined by square footage. An additional $50.00 will be charged for each individual living in the home who wants a spiritual healing. Travel time extra.

6. Magnetic Grid Balancing and Blessing of Your Home. Fee determined by square footage. Travel time extra. (Also available by phone)

7. Magnetic Grid Balancing and Blessing on Commercial Property. Fee determined by square footage. Travel time extra. (Also available by phone)

8. Releasing Back Stress for Expectant Mothers and Blessing of Their Baby.

9. Consultation for Special Needs Available.

Spiritual Strength

MY HEALING JOURNAL

UNCONDITIONAL LOVE

Hope

MY HEALING JOURNAL

UNCONDITIONAL LOVE

Humanity's Spiritual Plague

MY HEALING JOURNAL

UNCONDITIONAL LOVE

Body, Mind and Spirit Healing Center
Whittier, CA

HOW TO FIND THE BODY, MIND AND SPIRIT HEALING CENTER

Visit our website:

www.victorbarron.com

Email:

godbmshc@earthlink.net

Phone:

(562) 696-9544

Fax:

(562) 698-2399

Training Center

BODY, MIND AND SPIRIT HEALING CENTER
6347 FRIENDS AVE., WHITTIER, CA 90601, U.S.A. (562) 696-9544

Name: ____

Address: ____

City, State & Zip: __________________________________

Phone: (   ) ______________________ Email: ______________________

Please check off anything that may be of interest to you and mail to address above:

___ Attunement
___ Candle Healing
___ Chakra Harmonizing
___ Color Vibration Workshop
___ Embrace Yourself and Meet Your Guardian Angel
___ Book Order
___ Unfoldings
___ Private Session
___ Hands-On Spiritual Healing
___ Knowing and Working with Spirit Guides
___ Leech Removal
___ Magnetic Grid Balancing and Corrections
___ Traditional Shaman Healing
___ Phone Session
___ Meditations
___ Spiritual Retreat (Sweatlodge)

BODY, MIND AND SPIRIT HEALING CENTER
6347 FRIENDS AVE., WHITTIER, CA 90601, U.S.A. (562) 696-9544

Name: ____

Address: ____

City, State & Zip: __________________________________

Phone: (   ) ______________________ Email: ______________________

Please check off anything that may be of interest to you and mail to address above:

___ Attunement
___ Candle Healing
___ Chakra Harmonizing
___ Color Vibration Workshop
___ Embrace Yourself and Meet Your Guardian Angel
___ Book Order
___ Unfoldings
___ Private Session
___ Hands-On Spiritual Healing
___ Knowing and Working with Spirit Guides
___ Leech Removal
___ Magnetic Grid Balancing and Corrections
___ Traditional Shaman Healing
___ Phone Session
___ Meditations
___ Spiritual Retreat (Sweatlodge)